The Seventeenth Annual
National Exhibition of
Illustration held in the
Galleries of the
Society of Illustrators
128 East 63rd Street,
New York
February 12 through
April 18, 1975

ILLUSTRATORS 17

ILLUSTRATORS 17

Designed by Mal Bessen,
David Ng, S. Neil Fujita
Edited by
Roland Descombes

Hastings House, Publishers, Inc.
New York 10016

Contents

Illustrators 17 Committee:

Chairman:	Roland Descombes
Assistant Chairman:	Warren Rogers
Designer of Call for Entries and Announcement:	Bill Baffa
Illustrator for Call for Entries and Announcement:	Ray Ameijide
Hanging Chairmen:	Mitchell Hooks Walter Hortens
Treasurer:	John Witt
Editor of Annual Book:	Roland Descombes
Designers of Annual Book:	Mal Bessen David Ng S. Neil Fujita
Coordinator:	Arpi Ermoyan
Staff:	Terry Brown Anna Lee Fuchs Cathy Groff Andrea Herrick Jamie Musselman Norma Pimsler

ISBN: 8038-3401-2 Library of Congress Catalog Card Number: 59-10849 Printed in the United States of America

Distributors:
CANADA Saunders of Toronto Ltd., Don Mills, Ontario
GREAT BRITAIN Transatlantic Book Service, Ltd., 7 Maiden Lane, London WC2E 7NA
AUSTRIA, GERMANY AND SWITZERLAND Arthur Niggli, Ltd., Bohl, 9052 Niederteufen AR, Switzerland
FRANCE Editions Paralleles, 172 rue Pelleport, Paris XXe
All other countries Fleetbooks c/o Feffer and Simons, Inc., 100 Park Avenue, New York, NY 10017

The President's Message

Every year the Society of Illustrators gathers its energy, and gets together the means to produce the Annual National Exhibition of Illustration. A chairman is selected, designers, illustrators, jurors chosen, and our house staff gears up to work even harder.

And each time the show goes up on the walls of our gallery, people agree that the artwork is the best ever.

The magic that takes place between blank paper or canvas and an illustrator seems to be boundless. It is evident that if the market-place poses a problem, and gives the illustrator the freedom to solve it, the catalyst of paint, ink, dedicated labor and love never fail to produce a work unmatched in creativity and craftsmanship.

I congratulate all the fine illustrators whose artwork makes this exhibition a continuing landmark in our culture.

Alvin J. Pimsler, President

The Chairman/Editor's Statement

The Society of Illustrators Annual Show and the book which follows each show, is the only important showplace for illustration in the world today.

For me it has been an inspiration and an honor to have been the chairman of this year's show.

Roland L. Descombes

The Designer's Statement

I think the main reason designers would be interested in putting an Annual like this together is that they love seeing, working with, and being surrounded by first class art. And there are many fine examples of the best of American art in this unique and beautiful 17th edition.

Never mind the more than 1,000 man hours it took to design and lay out this Annual. All of us, Mal and David especially, feel that it gave us an opportunity to see what is really happening in the field. Above all, this Annual reaffirms our belief that in the creation of art for industry, as in no other category of art, the illustrator stands uniquely alone as a true individual creator of images.

It is a pleasure to see the growth in creativity and professionalism in so many of the illustrators we know and have worked with for many years. The trendsetters whose work is represented here are constantly changing and trying new techniques in their creative concepts. They never stop.

The 17th Annual should be especially noteworthy, since it comes out in the year of the Bicentennial. If art, whether it is done for industry or other areas, can act as a reflection of the quality of American life after 200 years, the illustrators must certainly be proud of this exhibition of their accomplishments and contributions.

S. Neil Fujita

Norman Rockwell

A Toast to Wesley McKeown from The Society of Illustrators President's Dinner 1975

…And now I would like to mention one who greatly enjoyed these evenings, but is not with us tonight. It is still difficult for me to believe we have lost the deeply involved, charismatic warmth of Wes McKeown. I would suspect you share my feelings.

This Society, that first rejected his application for membership only later to elect him its President, owes him a considerable debt for his many efforts on our behalf.

Rather than by reciting a litany of all his accomplishments, both in and out of the Society of Illustrators, a more concise indication of his continuing commitment may be discerned from the fact that five years after his tenure as President, when most former Presidents have greatly reduced their Society activities, Wes was photographing portraits of the entire membership for the upstairs gallery, was Chairman of the Air Force and Government Services Committee, arranging for membership changes, and serving on the Hall of Fame Committee….No doubt I am forgetting some activities, it is not easy to keep an accurate account of all he was doing.

Therefore, a toast to Wesley McKeown…Wes out there somewhere. Probably recording this event on tape and with four Nikons.

To Wes you were a heck of a man,
With love from the Society of Illustrators

Shannon Stirnweis, President 1972-74

Newark School of Fine
   and Industrial Arts 1950
U.S. Army 1945-47
Membership Chairman,
   Society of Illustrators
Air Force Chairman,
   Society of Illustrators
Treasurer, Society of Illustrators
Vice President, Society of Illustrators
President, Society of Illustrators
Dutch Treat Club
Recipient of the Silver Medal—
   Nikon International Award
   —Tokyo, Japan 1970
Paintings:
   U.S. Army Historical Collection
   U.S. Air Force Art Collection
   U.S. Navy Combat Art
   Prize Benedictine Art Awards 1969
Professional Illustrator 1950-1975

Hamilton King Award

Carol Anthony

I am one of those people who laughed at the Uncle Remus story Where Br'er Rabbit tried to talk to the tar baby and ended up all in a tangle with the speechless figure. I am also the person who was laughed at when I approached Carol Anthony's linen-maché "Algonquin Man," who was seated in the Society's gallery as part of Illustrators 17. I said, "I am sorry but the gallery is closing, sir. You'll have to leave." Needless to say, I received the same answer as Br'er Rabbit.

Carol Anthony, a native New Yorker and graduate of the Rhode Island School of Design, is one of the Society of Illustrators' brightest young stars. She is the recipient of the 1975 Hamilton King Award for her "Algonquin Man" commissioned by Andrew Kner of the New York Times. This award is named after the self-taught and highly respected illustrator of the 1900's and has been given annually since 1965 for the best illustration of the year by a member of the Society.

Carol has achieved tremendous success with her three-dimensional figures since their showing at the Museum of Contemporary Crafts in New York City in 1967. This exhibit travelled for two years under the auspices of the Smithsonian Institution. This led to exhibits at the Bienville Gallery of New Orleans, the Lyman Allyn Museum of New London, Connecticut, the Xerox Gallery in Rochester, and the Fairtree and Young & Rubicam Galleries in New York. Her works have also been exhibited in Switzerland and Colombia, South America.

The characters evolve from a prop, often a pair of old shoes, Carol's personal observations, insights and imagination. The procedure is her own and the final solution as secret as a formula for rocket fuel. Her "friends" include Giuseppi, the fruit vendor; Fred, the plumber; Babes in carriages; Codgers; The Old General; Queenie, the dancer; Rugby George and an entire Little League team. Carol's works are in the collections of the Hirshorn Museum and the New Orleans Museum of Art.

A member of the Society of Illustrators since 1970, Carol has had a one-woman show at the Society and been exhibited in its Annual Show. She presently lives and works in her home in Greenwich, Connecticut.

The Hall of Fame Awards

Bernard Fuchs

Travelling east from St. Louis, Missouri, some fifty miles into rural Illinois, one approaches O'Fallon in St. Clair County. One is immediately struck by the absence of an historical marker noting this small town as the birthplace of Bernard Fuchs, recipient of the Society of Illustrators Hall of Fame award for 1975.

Bernie's professional art training began at the School of Fine Art at Washington University in St. Louis. His style was developed in the studios of Detroit, where his illustrations for automobile ads were an immediate success. This popularity was noted by the magazine publishers in New York, whose assignments brought Bernie national recognition. This success prompted a move to Westport, Connecticut, the artists' colony on Long Island Sound. Bernie had married his childhood neighbor, the former Anna Lee Hesse, and they have three children; Derek, Ellise and Cindy.

He has been awarded a total of three Gold Medals from the Society of Illustrators Annual Exhibitions. He was elected "Artist of the Year" by the Artists Guild of New York in 1962 and received the Hamilton King Award from the Society in 1966.

He has had several one-man shows in New York and Westport and was part of the United States Information Agency's Graphics Exhibition in 1963.

Fluid and evocative are words often used to describe his style. Bernie adds, "it took a long time to develop that, to really study and control looseness." He used this style very remarkably in a recent reportage portfolio of English pubs for Lithopinion, a magazine which has allowed him a free hand to travel and paint such varied events as the races at Longchamps in Paris and the running of the bulls in Pamplona, Spain. His work has also taken him to London, Central America, the Caribbean Islands, including Cuba.

A member of the Society of Illustrators since 1959, Bernie has served on several juries for their Annual Exhibitions. He is frequently asked to jury exhibitions around the country and to lecture as well. He was part of the Society's lecture series in 1973 and 1975.

Howard Pyle

The Quaker gentleman of Wilmington, who carried American Illustration from the days of wood engravings into the modern era of four color reproduction, may have made his strongest influence on American art in the classroom and not on the drawing board. Howard Pyle's reputation as an instructor was as widespread as his reputation for the heroic tales and adventures represented in his writings and illustrations. He was a hard driving instructor, as the letters of his students proclaim. It was this drive itself which lifted many wavering young artists at the turn of the century and carried their names to editors and honor rolls. His style of instruction was for the dedicated and talented only. Howard Pyle was a prolific author as well as artist, continuing his writings during his entire professional career.

The farm country surrounding

Wilmington is one of the nation's richest in Quaker tradition. The first settlers of the area brought firm beliefs and family ties to the area. Such were the roots of young Howard Pyle, oldest son of William and Margaret Pyle, born on May 5, 1853. Howard was able, at age 16, to commute to Philadelphia to study under European Prof. Van der Weilen. This instruction was primarily in technique and after three years he had mastered the course. It was his own personal study which he knew was shaping his style. His interest in American history and costume and his lingering feelings on the value of the famous European masters were uppermost in his research.

He met Anne Poole at a church function and they were married in Quaker fashion. They had seven children as the family outgrew two houses in burgeoning Wilmington. Howard worked in his studio on

Franklin Street from 1883 and in 1900 rebuilt the structure to accommodate his new school. The family summered at Rehobeth Beach, Delaware and Howard was a weekend commuter there. His lifestyle became routine, but his energies never diminished. He would write and draw for 12 hours a day and relax only on weekends. A list of his published works is extensive, but he never enjoyed the financial ease that the upcoming illustrators of the early 1900's had.

The final project that Howard Pyle embarked on began in 1910, when many of his friends and the best-known artists of the day were being commissioned to do murals and large panel paintings. He was new to this and his studio would not accommodate it. His friends were returning from Europe where they had large studio space for this type of work. It was decided that the family would spend a year in Italy, with the boys, then at Yale, joining them when they could. It was his only trip abroad. He died in Florence a year later having completed only one mural.

The use of half tones and color plate reproductions were the biggest developments of the era. Howard did his first work for color reproduction in 1881 for Dodd, Mead & Co. and was very dissatisfied. As he was the foremost illustrator of the day, he was the first to be asked to try the new methods. By 1902 the process was able to reproduce colors accurately and Howard Pyle's vivd imagination for color had its full freedom. He seldom used the pen again and his color paintings appeared in Harper's Monthly and Scribner's. It also gave a more realistic feeling to his adventure stories.

He spent the summers of 1898 and 1899 at Chadd's Ford in the Brandywine Valley, where he had begun instructions for selected students, paid for by the Drexel Institute. It was a beautiful area rich in scenic vistas for drawing and painting. He came to realize that these classes, open and unregimented, were the only true method of instruction. They became the start of his own school in the rebuilt studio on Franklin Street in 1901. Select students from the art schools on the East coast were accepted. There was minimal scheduling and few fees. He mixed a weekly critique and instruction with studio time for each student. The students soon found that mere mention of Howard Pyle's name would open doors that years of experience would not.

He always stressed to his students to live in the world of their subjects, to feel the emotions of their characters and to see life through their eyes. His Wilmington and his school was his own fairy-tale reality.

Photo: Keystone Press Agency. Courtesy
The World Book Encyclopedia

Maxfield Parrish

Maxfield Parrish's glowing landscapes and beautiful visions of sun-
light and moonlight, his figures
radiating the simple, almost angelic,
postures of life were the trademark
of an artist at the top of the illustration field at the turn of the century.
His larger-than-life villains and
smaller-than-life figures in landscapes flowed freely from the vivid
imagination of a simple man,
straightforward in his outlook on
life. To capture the single sunbeam
which would reflect the beauty of
the world as he saw it and to pass
that beam through a prism of color
was his style. He was alone in its
mastery and it earned him the
respect and recognition of the art
world and the viewing public across
the globe.

The first child of Stephen Parrish, a
Philadelphia shopkeeper and
talented artist, and his wife, Eliza-
beth, was Frederick, born on July
25, 1870. He later took his maternal
grandmother's maiden name,
Maxfield, and was known as such
his entire professional career. He
was a young man, curious about
life and blessed with an artistic
talent encouraged by his father.
The many influences on the young
Parrish shaped the man of gen-
erosity and love, and the artist of
grace and dedication.

The Parrish family were Quakers;
and although Maxfield was not a
practicing member, this Quaker
background stressing hard work
and sacrifice, developed the quali-
ties he maintained throughout his
whole life. However, his religious
background did hinder his formal
education. Art was not considered
a worthwhile field of study at Haver-
ford College, the Quaker institution
where he enrolled to study archi-
tecture in 1888. He later withdrew
from the Society of Friends, the
Quaker church to which he belonged

by birth, when he married outside that society.

Maxfield began his formal art training at the Pennsylvania Academy of the Fine Arts in Philadelphia. He studied there until 1894 while working at his father's studio in Annisquam, Mass., and later at his father's home, "Northcote," built in 1893, in the Connecticut River Valley town of Cornish, N.H. These were favorite spots of solitude for Maxfield in his early days of study.

He began his long and productive commercial career in Philadelphia where he occupied studios until 1898. However, his need for uninterrupted work time and his love of the Connecticut Valley countryside prompted him to build a home, "The Oaks" in Windsor, Vt. on the New Hampshire border across the valley from his father's home in Cornish. Maxfield's wife, the former Lydia Austin, an art instructor he met while auditing a class of Howard Pyle's at the Drexel Institute in Philadelphia, raised four children at "The Oaks"—John, Maxfield, Jr., Stephen and Jean. "The Oaks" was a favorite stop in the summer for the intellectuals who lived in the "Cornish Colony," as the picturesque valley came to be known. In the winter it was often snowbound. Maxfield flourished in this atmosphere of seclusion for his work and an open social life amongst his friends.

Maxfield had established his reputation with his magazine and children's book illustrations, as well as his poster work of the 1890's. He became much in demand for advertising work. However, advertising art became more of a burden to Maxfield who disliked the "men with good intentions" who were a constant distraction. He preferred to make his pictures for reproductions as calendars and art prints.

Art prints of his works had been available since 1904 but by the 1920's the demand was so great that The House of Art in New York began to commission his works specifically for reproduction in great volume. His calendars for the Edison Mazda Lamp division of the General Electric Company, the one advertising client with whom he had a lasting relationship, were so popular that over a million reproductions were sold each year and became his primary artform for many years. His relationship with The House of Art lasted until 1928 and he painted his last Edison Mazda calendar in 1934. During Maxfield's last 30 years as an artist, he painted landscapes exclusively. Many were reproduced in print form by the Brown and Bigelow Company, a major calendar distributor.

From Maxfield Parrish by Coy Ludwig. Reprinted by permission of Watson-Guptill Publications.

The First 75 Years of the Society

The opening section of our Constitution states in part that its purpose is "To promote and stimulate interest in the art of illustration, past, present and future, and to give impetus generally toward high ideals in the art by means of exhibitions, lectures, educational programs, social intercourse, and in such other ways as may seem advisable."

The Society of Illustrators is 75 years old.

It seems appropriate that in this Annual, our 17th, we talk a bit about why the Society is uniquely important in our profession. It is important not because it has existed for 75 years, but because it has lived up to its original mandate. It has kept its eye on the ball.

Indeed, the Annual National Exhibition, and this book, is but one of many manifestations of dedication by members of the Society to those lofty goals. It must be noted that virtually every project of the Society works for the entire profession, not just for its members.

A true history of the 75 years would take many pages and, in this "picture book," it might not be widely read. So this will be a mere itemized list with explanatory notes. It may prove to be a bit of proud drumbeating—sometimes quite out of chronological order.

At the outset, in 1901, men like Charles Dana Gibson, Edward Penfield, Williams Glackens, Everett Shinn, Daniel Carter Beard, Dean Cornwell and Wallace Morgan met in then-famous restaurants like the Brevoort, Lafayette and Mouquins to discuss their profession and socialize. By 1903 they had progressed to the point of adopting a constitution.

With the coming of World War I many illustrators went overseas while others on the home front formed a committee to produce billboards, posters, advertising and editorial drawings—everything to promote the war effort, sell Liberty Bonds and the like. They met at Keen's Chop House, under chairman Gibson, to receive their assignments. James Montgomery Flagg's famous Uncle Sam's "I Want You" poster was painted at this time.

Incorporation took place in 1921 but it was not until 1935 that the Society rented, and renovated, an old blacksmith's shop at 128 West 24th Street as its first clubhouse.

By 1939 that building was too small, so after a long search a stable (actually, a carriage house) was found at 128 East 63rd Street. And that is where we are now—bursting at the seams in support of all our many projects. In 1949 the mortgage was paid off. Wonder of wonders!

World War II brought action again for the illustrators, in and out of uniform. Naturally, there were many artist-correspondents. One project: each week a group of members were flown in a B-29 to military hospitals all over the country to do portraits of the wounded and disabled. These works were brought back to New York where volunteers matted and mailed them to mothers wives or sweethearts. In all, the incredible number of 64,000 portraits were done for which the Society received a citation from the Department of Defense.

In 1945 the Society, along with the Art Directors Club and the Artists Guild, joined to establish the Joint Ethics Committee and formulate the "Code of Fair Practice." The committee is now sponsored by other groups as well and is a strong voice in upholding the ethical standards set forth in the Code.

The Society of Illustrators in 1954 collaborated with the newly designated United States Air Force in setting up an art program to record Air Force activities and history. This program, under which artists have traveled to every area of the world where we have air bases, has produced over 1,000 paintings by over 150 artists. One aspect of Air Force history we are proud to have recorded are the hundreds of humanitarian activities carried out in Central America, Turkey, North Africa, Pakistan, by Hungarian Airlift, the German Kinderlift and others. After a few years of being totally a New York operation, the program was expanded to Los Angeles and San Francisco Societies. We have also worked with the Parks Department (U.S. Department of the Interior) under a similar program.

Educationally, the Society of Illustrators has been involved in so many projects that a full listing is impossible in this space. There are yearly lecture series for students and professionals; portfolio reviews; drawing, painting and portrait classes; visiting lecturers in high schools; a program of visiting artists at the State Training School for Boys at Warwick, N.Y.; and more.

Year in and year out the Society Galleries offer a continuous program of exhibitions of the best in illustration. These are open to the public at no charge. Included, of course, is our Annual National Exhibition from which this book originates.

The Society's Hall of Fame has set about to honor top American illustrators both living and dead. To date, 28 artists have been so honored.

Each year there is a student competition with entries submitted from over 80 accredited art schools from 44 states. The 22 cash awards are given to further the art education of the recipients. The Society supports these competitions by an Annual Christmas Art Sale with additional help coming from some outside sources, most notably the Reader's Digest Foundation.

Another Society fund with a most serious purpose is that administered by the Welfare Committee. The mandate is to help artists, on a temporary basis, if there has been a financial setback due to illness, accident or in some cases just a difficult financial period. The recipient does not have to be a member of the Society of Illustrators. This fund was until recent years supported totally by what were called the S.I. Girlie Shows. Those rather racy reviews were held annually, first in the Hecksher Theater and later in the Society's own theater. Many famous illustrators either starred in the production, wrote the material, or designed and painted the sets.

Some years back the Society established an Achievement Award given to people of distinction in affinity professions. Only four people have been awarded this coveted recognition: Sidney L. James, first publisher of Sports Illustrated; Colonel George C. Bales, USAF, co-creator of the Air Force art program; Herbert R. Mayes, renowned publisher and editor of several major American magazines; and Edward Swayduck, ex-president of Local One, Amalgamated Lithographers Union, a labor statesman and sponsor of good design and illustration.

Well, that's the record. We, of the Society look to the future with confidence. It may be even better than the first 75 years.

Robert Geissmann

ILLUSTRATORS 17

Juries

Advertising

Howard Munce, Chairman
Milton Charles
Ken Longtemps
Jerry Pinkney
Richard Hess
Blake Hampton
Sandy Kossin
David K. Stone

Editorial

David Blossom, Chairman
Bernie Karlin
Tom Daly
Guy Billout
Mike Palumbo
Bart Forbes
Marie Michel
Howard Sanden
Bob Peak

Book

Doug Johnson, Chairman
Les Thompson
Alan E. Cober
Rupert Finegold
Larry Kresek
Chris Duke
Howard Rogers
Harry Schaare

Institutional

Mike Hooks, Chairman
Paul Calle
Marylin Hafner
Peter Schaumann
Bobbi Pearlman
Tony Saris
Don Hedin

Film

Bernie Fuchs, Chairman
Bob Handville
Chuck Adorney
Doris Rodewig
Al Pisano

2
Advertising
Artist: **Jack Endewelt**
Art Director: Anthony Hilliard
Agency: Compton Advertising Agency
Client: Iberian Airlines of Spain

3
Institutional
Artist: **Alan E. Cober**
Art Director: Milton Simpson/Gretchen Ackerman
Agency: Johnson/Simpson
Client: Conoco

PRESIDENT NIXON HIDING IN A SMALL TOWN

4
Editorial
Artist: **Dennis Corrigan**
Art Director: Dennis Corrigan

5
Book
Artist: **Richard Anderson**
Art Director: Ian Summers
Title: The Gift
Publisher: Ballantine Books, Inc.

6
Advertising
Artist: **Fred Otnes**
Art Director: Allen Seide
Agency: Allen Seide Advertising, Inc.
Client: Finch Paper

8
Editorial
Artist: **Dickran Palulian**
Art Director: Joe Brooks
Publication: Penthouse Magazine

7
Editorial
Artist: **Bill Nelson**
Art Director: Steve Phillips
Publication: New Times Magazine

9
Advertising
Artist: **Bernie Fuchs**
Art Director: Jack Marinelli
Agency: Leisure Marketing Services
Client: Winchester-Western

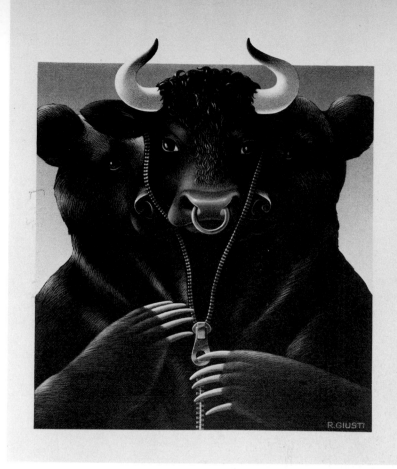

10
Editorial
Artist: **Robert Giusti**
Art Director: Herbert Rosenthal
Publication: Institutional Investor

11
Advertising
Artist: **Al Hirshfeld**
Art Director: John Berg
Client: CBS Records

CHARLES IVES

THE 100TH ANNIVERSARY

1874 – 1974

Richard Hess

13
Editorial
Artist: **Joe Ciardiello**
Art Director: Joe Ciardiello

12
Advertising
Artist: **Richard Hess**
Art Director: Henrietta Condak
Client: CBS Records

15
Editorial
Artist: **Alan E. Cober**
Art Director: Joseph Csatari
Publication: Boys' Life Magazine
Gold Medal

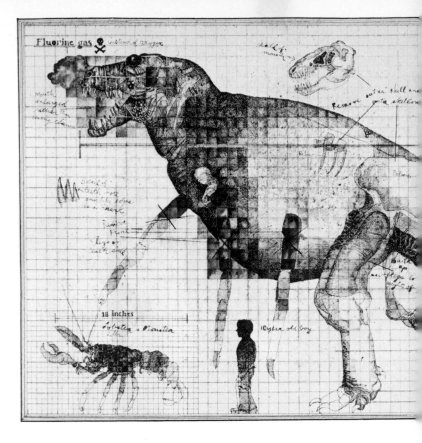

14
Book
Artist: **Philip Castle**
Art Director: David Pelham
Title: The John Lennon Song Book
Publisher: Penguin Books

16
Institutional
Artist: **Carol Bouman**
Art Director: Carol Bouman
Client: Charles White Ltd.

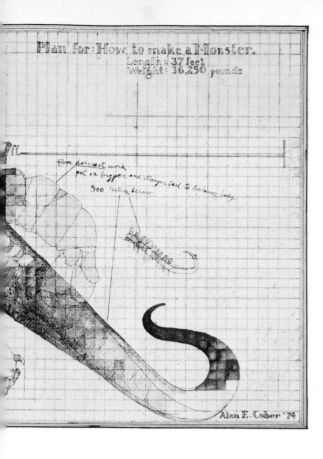

17
Editorial
Artist: **Bernie Fuchs**
Art Director: Richard Gangel
Publication: Sports Illustrated

18
Institutional
Artist: **Tony Eubanks**
Art Director: Tony Eubanks

19
Institutional
Artist: **Carol Anthony**
Art Director: Carl Herrman
Client: The Literary Guild
Gold Medal

20
Advertising
Artist: **Bernie Fuchs**
Art Director: Mike Palombo
Agency: Norman Affiliates
Client: Westvaco

21
Advertising
Artist: **Peter Lloyd**
Art Director: Frank Mulvey
Client: RCA Records

22
Institutional
Artist: **Raymond Ameijide**
Art Director: Bill Baffa
Client: Society of Illustrators, Inc.

23
Advertising
Artist: **Richard Amsel**
Art Director: Joseph Stelmach
Client: RCA Records

24
Book
Artist: **David Blossom**
Art Director: Thomas Von Der Linn
Title: I, Benedict Arnold
Publisher: The Reader's Digest

25
Book
Artist: **David Blossom**
Art Director: Thomas Von Der Linn
Title: I, Benedict Arnold
Publisher: The Reader's Digest

26
Book
Artist: **Philip Castle**
Art Director: Philip Castle
Title: Elvis Complete
Publisher: Music Sales Ltd.

27
Institutional
Artist: **Bob Lapsley**
Art Director: Niel Gulley
Client: Baroid Division/NL Industries

28
Editorial
Artist: **Garie Blackwell**
Art Director: Linda Cox
Publication: Cosmopolitan

29
Book
Artist: **Kenneth Francis Dewey**
Art Director: Jean Harley Reese
Title: Look With May Ling
Publisher: Ginn and Company

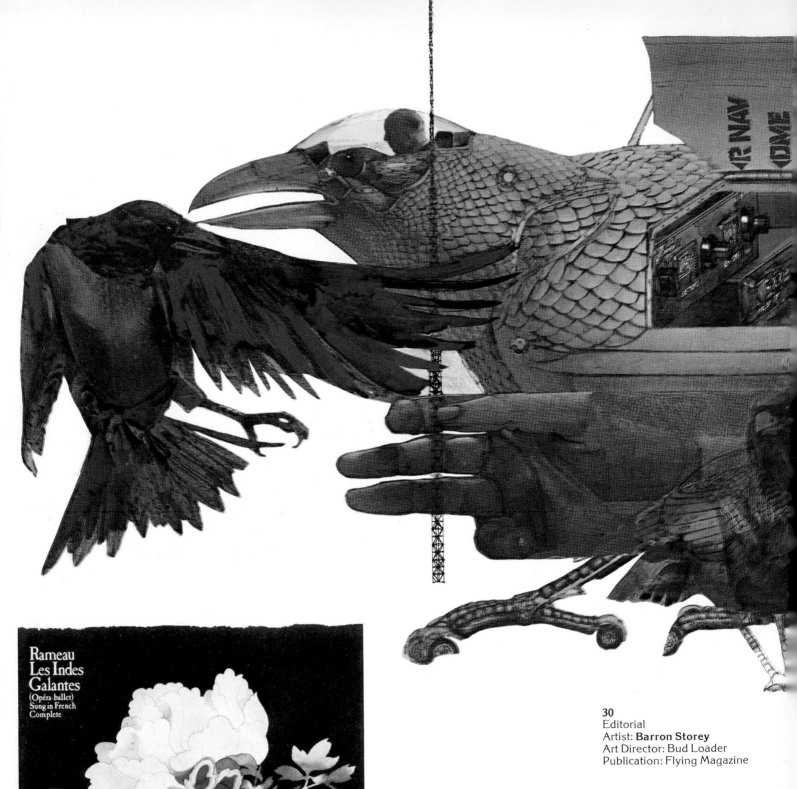

30
Editorial
Artist: **Barron Storey**
Art Director: Bud Loader
Publication: Flying Magazine

Rameau
Les Indes
Galantes
(Opéra-ballet)
Sung in French
Complete

Soloists·Ensemble Vocal
Raphaël Passaquet
La Grande Ecurie
Et La Chambre Du Roy
Jean-Claude Malgoire,
Conductor

31
Advertising
Artist: **Milton Glaser**
Art Director: John Berg
Client: CBS Records

32
Editorial
Artist: **Richard Harvey**
Art Director: Bernard Springsteel
Publication: Good Housekeeping

33
Book
Artist: **James Bama**
Art Director: Leonard Leone
Title: The Killers
Publisher: Bantam Books, Inc.

34
Television
Artist: **Bill Hofmann**
Art Director: Dolores Gudzin
Client: NBC Television Network

35
Book
Artist: **Herb Tauss**
Art Director: Richard M. Kapelsohn
Title: The Snowman
Publisher: Manor Books Inc.

36
Advertising
Artist: **Bob McGuiness**
Art Director: Barry Kaufman/Rich LoMonaco
Agency: Communications Quorum, Inc.
Client: United Artists Corp.

37
Advertising
Artist: **Mark English**
Art Director: Anthony V. Leone
Agency: Lewis & Gilman Advertising
Client: Roerig/Pfizer Pharmaceuticals

38
Advertising
Artist: **Peter Lloyd**
Art Director: Bob Defrin
Client: Atlantic Records

39
Book
Artist: **David Passalacqua**
Art Director: Leonard Leone
Title: American Preview 20
Publisher: Bantam Books, Inc.

40
Television
Artist: **Robert Giusti**
Art Director: Gail Plautz
Client: CBS Television Network

41
Television
Artist: **Robert Heindel**
Art Director: Dolores Gudzin
Client: NBC Television Network

42
Advertising
Artist: **Barron Storey**
Art Director: Robert Hall
Agency: Dean L. Burdick Associates, Inc.
Client: Winthrop Laboratories

43
Editorial
Artist: **Bob Peak**
Art Director: Richard Gangel
Publication: Sports Illustrated

44
Book
Artist: **Charles Moll**
Art Director: Milton Charles
Title: The Sodom and Gomorrah Business
Publisher: Pocket Books

45
Book
Artist: **Michael Horen**
Art Director: Judie Mills
Title: Auto Mechanics
Publisher: Franklin Watts, Inc.

46
Editorial
Artist: **Wilson McLean**
Art Director: Don Menell/George Kenton
Publication: Oui Magazine

47
Advertising
Artist: **John Ward**
Art Director: John Ward

48
Advertising
Artist: **Alex Gnidziejko**
Art Director: Leslie Sisman
Agency: Frank J. Corbett, Inc.
Client: G.D. Searle International Co.

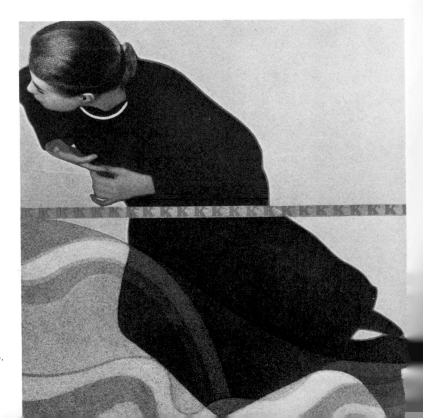

49
Editorial
Artist: **Peter Lloyd**
Art Director: Tom Gould
Publication: Psychology Today

50
Advertising
Artist: **Larry Noble**
Art Director: Larry Noble
Client: Mulvey Associates

51
Advertising
Artist: **Melinda Borderlon**
Art Director: Bob Defrin
Client: Big Tree Records

52
Advertising
Artist: **Bruce Wolfe**
Art Director: John Immel
Agency: Klemtner Advertising
Client: Syntex Laboratories

53
Editorial
Artist: **Terry Steadham**
Art Director: Dean Eller
Publication: Holiday Magazine

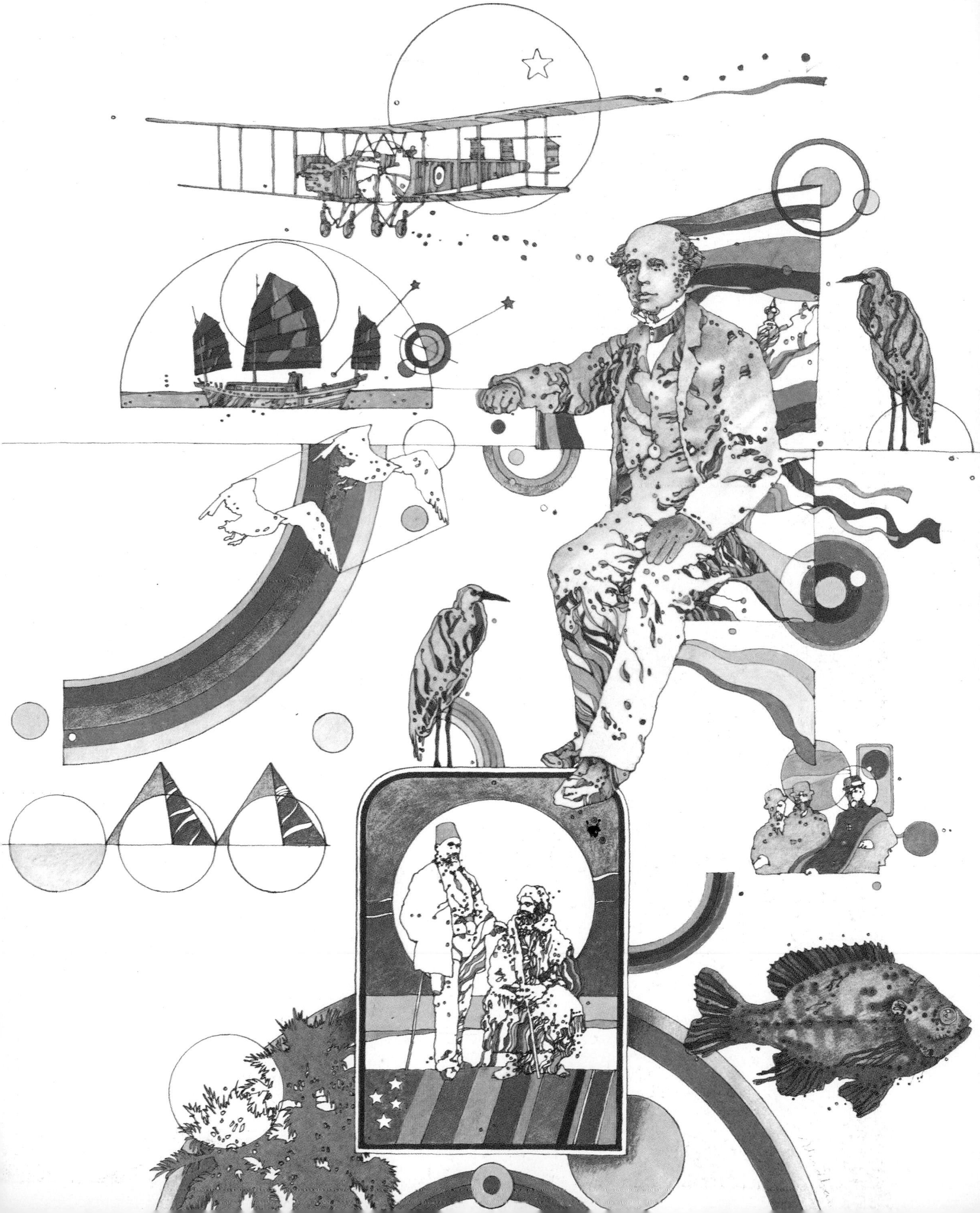

54
Advertising
Artist: **Clifford Andree**
Art Director: Jack Byrne
Agency: Ford, Byrne & Associates
Client: Insurance Co. of North America

56
Institutional
Artist: **Holly Hobbie**
Art Director: Ray Kowalski
Client: American Greetings Corp.

55
Advertising
Artist: **Wendell Minor**
Art Director: Kent Salisbury
Agency: Salisbury Associates
Client: Cue Magazine

57
Advertising
Artist: **Gary R. Radtke**
Art Director: Gary R. Radtke
Client: Maywood & Hammer, Inc.

59
Advertising
Artist: **Clifford Andree**
Art Director: Jack Byrne
Agency: Ford, Byrne & Associates
Client: Insurance Co. of North America

58
Book
Artist: **Olivia H.H. Cole**
Art Director: Olivia H.H. Cole

60
Institutional
Artist: **Fred Otnes**
Art Director: Tom Clemente/Lynn Moran
Client: Newspaper Advertising Bureau

62
Editorial
Artist: **George Jones**
Art Director: Marion Davis
Publication: The Reader's Digest

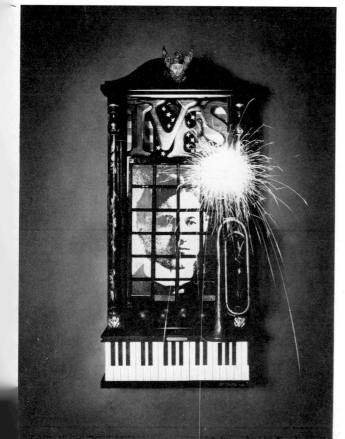

61
Advertising
Artist: **Jim Timmons**
Art Director: Joseph Stelmach
Client: RCA Records

63
Editorial
Artist: **Peter Lloyd**
Art Director: Don Menell/Rodney Williams
Publication: Oui Magazine

64
Editorial
Artist: **Andy Lackow**
Art Director: Armando Galvez
Publication: Gallery Magazine

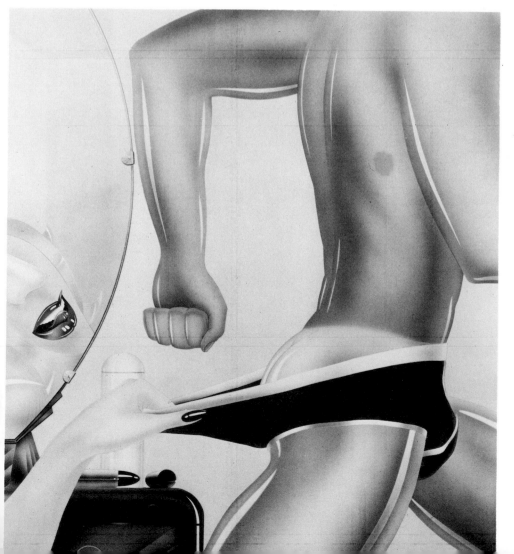

65
Editorial
Artist: **Peter Lloyd**
Art Director: Art Kane
Publication: Viva Magazine

66
Editorial
Artist: **Robert M. Cunningham**
Art Director: Tom Ries
Publication: The American Way

67
Editorial
Artist: **Guy Fery**
Art Director: William F. Cadge
Publication: Redbook

68
Book
Artist: **Bernard L. D'Andrea**
Art Director: Bernard L. D'Andrea

69
Editorial
Artist: **Bart Forbes**
Art Director: Vince Maiello
Client: The Literary Guild

70
Book
Artist: **John Keely**
Art Director: John Keely

71
Editorial
Artist: **Bart Forbes**
Art Director: B. Martin Pedersen
Publication: Pastimes Magazine

72A
Institutional
Artist: **Don Weller**
Art Director: Don Weller
Agency: The Weller Institute
Client: Southern California Edison

72
Institutional
Artist: **Don Weller**
Art Director: Don Weller
Agency: The Weller Institute
Client: Southern California Edison

73
Book
Artist: **Robert Grossman**
Art Director: Ian Summers
Title: Dark Star
Publisher: Ballantine Books, Inc.

74
Book
Artist: **Meg Birnbaum**
Art Director: Meg Birnbaum

75
Editorial
Artist: **Radjin**
Art Director: Norman S. Hotz
Publication: Travel & Leisure Magazine

76
Advertising
Artist: **David Palladini**
Art Director: Joe Fazio
Client: Geigy Pharmaceuticals

77
Book
Artist: **Guy Billout**
Art Director: Zlata Paces
Title: Poets Notice Everything
Publisher: Macmillan Publishing Co., Inc.

78
Book
Artist: **Robert Byrd**
Art Director: Riki Levinson
Title: Pinchpenny Mouse
Publisher: Windmill Books/E. P. Dutton & Co., Inc.

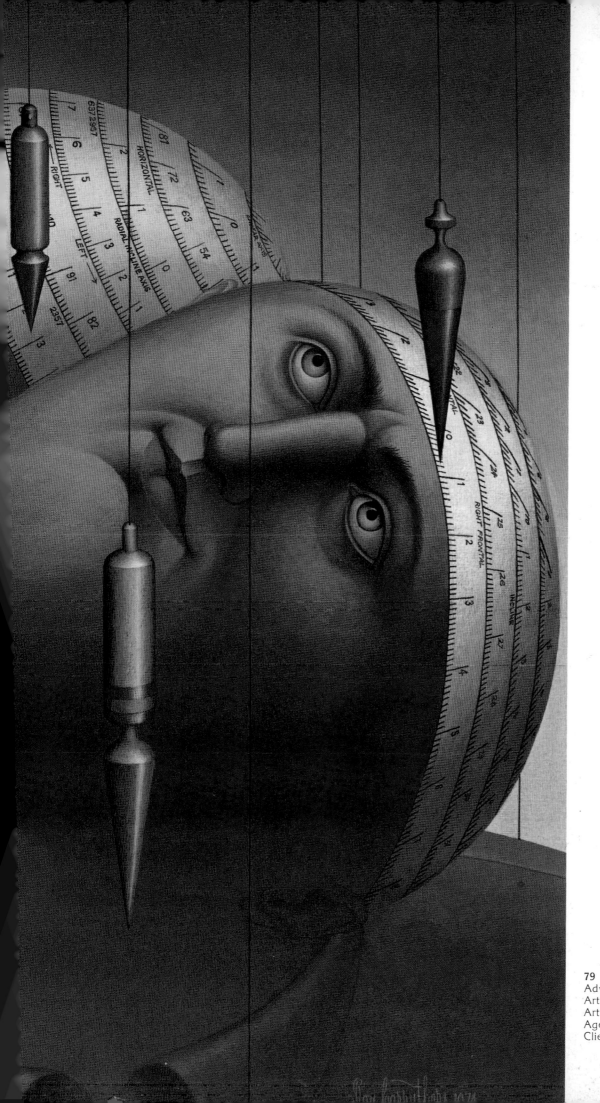

79
Advertising
Artist: **Roy Carruthers**
Art Director: Anthony V. Leone
Agency: Lewis & Gilman Advertising
Client: Roerig/Pfizer Pharmaceuticals

80
Book
Artist: **Kaaren Shandroff**
Art Director: Kaaren Shandroff

82
Book
Artist: **David McCall Johnston**
Art Director: David McCall Johnston

81
Editorial
Artist: **Siegbert Reinhard**
Art Director: Siegbert Reinhard

83
Editorial
Artist: **Edward Soyka**
Art Director: Ira Silberlicht/Tom Lennon
Publication: Emergency Medicine

84
Book
Artist: **Peter Schauman**
Art Director: Lidia Ferrara
Title: Snakehunter
Publisher: Random House, Inc.

85
Book
Artist: **Leo Dillon**
Art Director: Zlata Paces
Publisher: Macmillan Publishing Co., Inc.

I can button my own shirt.

86
Editorial
Artist: **Diane deGroat**
Art Director: Skip Sorvino
Publication: Scholastic Magazine

88
Book
Artist: **George S. Gaadt**
Art Director: Ilsa Berzins/Zlata Paces
Publisher: Macmillan Publishing Co., Inc.

87
Editorial
Artist: **Ann Raymo**
Art Director: Kenneth R. Hine
Publication: Creative Living Magazine

89
Editorial
Artist: **Chuck Wilkinson**
Art Director: Herb Bleiweiss/Bruce Danbrot
Publication: Ladies' Home Journal

91
Advertising
Artist: **Bill Nelson**
Art Director: Bill Nelson

90
Editorial
Artist: **Judith Jampel**
Art Director: Judith Jampel
Award for Excellence

92
Editorial
Artist: **Robert Grossman**
Art Director: Stan Braverman
Publication: Tennis Magazine

93
Advertising
Artist: **Shawn Shea**
Art Director: Peter Hesse
Agency: Peter Hesse Advertising, Inc.
Client: Scott Printing Co., Ltd.

94
Advertising
Artist: **Robert Weaver**
Art Director: John Berg
Client: CBS Records

95
Editorial
Artist: **Robert Baxter**
Art Director: Vince Maiello
Publication: The Literary Guild Magazine

Editorial
Artist: **Jeffrey W. Cornell**
Art Director: Burton P. Pollack
Publication: Patient Care

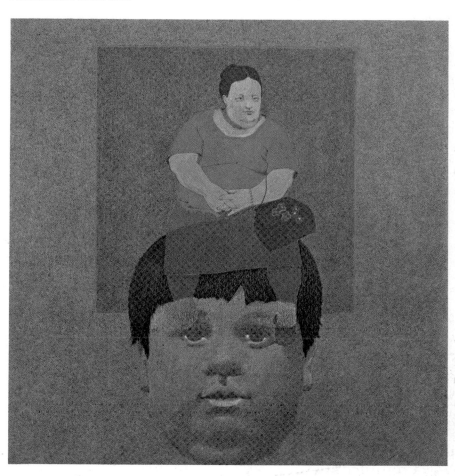

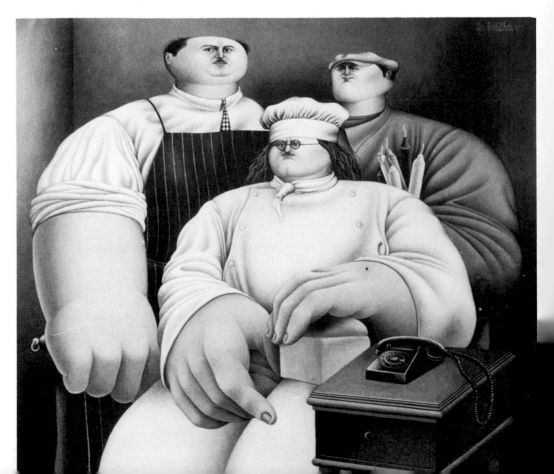

101
Editorial
Artist: **Mark English**
Art Director: John DeCesare/Joe Fazio
Publication: Diabetology '73

102
Advertising
Artist: **Robert C. Kinyon**
Art Director: Don Young/Jim Crouch
Agency: Don Young & Jim Crouch Graphic Design
Client: San Diego Gas & Electric Co.

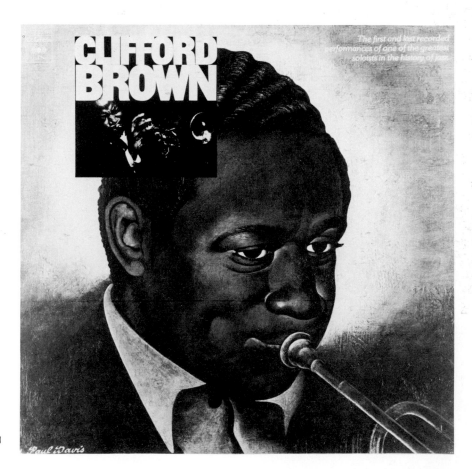

103
Advertising
Artist: **Paul Davis**
Art Director: John Berg
Client: CBS Records

104
Book
Artist: **George Ladas**
Art Director: George Ladas

105
Advertising
Artist: **Paul Giovanopoulos**
Art Director: B. Martin Pedersen
Agency: Pedersen Design, Inc.
Client: The New York Times

107
Advertising
Artist: **Ray Domingo**
Art Director: Pete Noto
Agency: Altman-Stoller Weiss Advertising, Inc.
Client: Wrangler Sport Wear

106
Advertising
Artist: **Paul Giovanopoulos**
Art Director: B. Martin Pedersen
Agency: Pedersen Design, Inc.
Client: The New York Times

108
Editorial
Artist: **James McMullan**
Art Director: Henry Wolf
Publication: Sesame St. Magazine

109
Institutional
Artist: **Ruth Brunner-Strosser**
Art Director: Ruth Brunner-Strosser
Client: Pitt Studios

110
Institutional
Artist: **Ruth Brunner-Strosser**
Art Director: Ruth Brunner-Strosser
Client: Pitt Studios

111
Advertising
Artist: **Gerry Gersten**
Art Director: Eliot Mancitto
Agency: N. W. Ayer International
Client: Union Dime Savings Bank

112
Advertising
Artist: **Charles Santore**
Art Director: Elmer Pizzi
Agency: Gray & Rogers, Inc.
Client: Grit

113
Editorial
Artist: **Donald Leake**
Art Director: Ron Barrett
Publication: Children's TV Workshop

114
Editorial
Artist: **Bernie Fuchs**
Art Director: Bob Crozier
Publication: Boy's Life Magazine

115
Book
Artist: **Paul Mann**
Art Director: Paul Mann

116
Editorial
Artist: **Bernie Fuchs**
Art Director: Bob Crozier
Publication: Boy's Life Magazine

117
Book
Artist: **Shannon Stirnweis**
Art Director: Shannon Stirnweis

118
Institutional
Artist: **Jack N. Unruh**
Art Director: Jerry McPhail
Agency: Bloom Advertising Agency
Client: Dallas/Fort Worth Society of
    Visual Communications

119
Advertising
Artist: **Joe Isom**
Art Director: Joe Isom

120
Institutional
Artist: **Jerry Pinkney**
Art Director: Jeff Raflaf
Agency: Fredrick Siebel Associates
Client: Seagram

121
Institutional
Artist: **Jerry Pinkney**
Art Director: Jeff Raflaf
Agency: Fredrick Siebel Associates
Client: Seagram

122
Institutional
Artist: **Gene Szafran**
Art Director: Gene Szafran
Client: Artists Associates
Award of Excellence

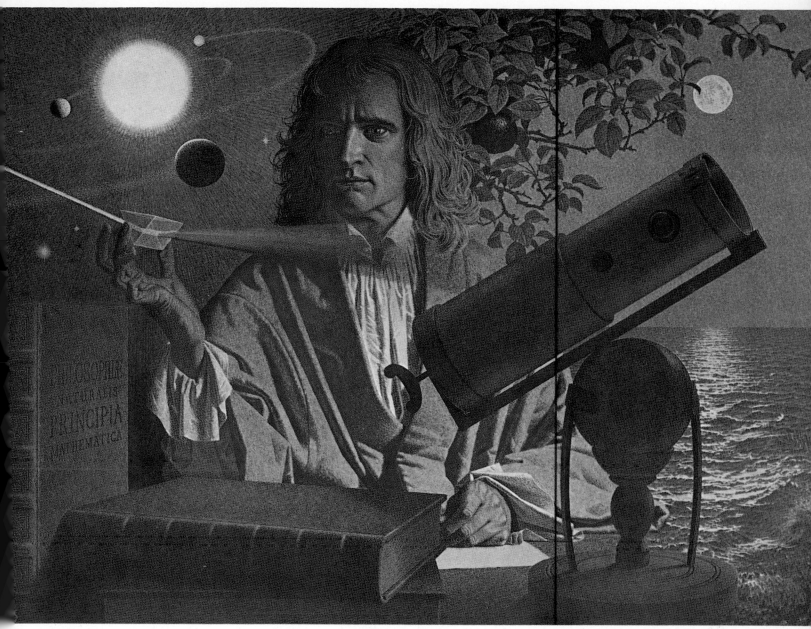

123
Editorial
Artist: **Jean Leon Huens**
Art Director: Howard E. Paine
Publication: National Geographic Magazine

124
Institutional
Artist: **Chet Jezierski**
Art Director: Art Kesten
Client: Army Aviation Association of
　　America

125
Editorial
Artist: **Julia Noonan**
Art Director: William F. Cadge
Publication: Redbook

126
Advertising
Artist: **David Kilmer**
Art Director: Angelo Sardina
Agency: Grant-Jacoby, Inc.
Client: Nekoosa-Edwards Paper Co.

127
Editoral
Artist: **Bunny Carter**
Art Director: Velveteen Rose
Publication: Womansports Magazine

128
Institutional
Artist: **Daniel Schwartz**
Art Director: Irwin Glusker
Agency: Irwin Glusker Associates
Client: Mobil Oil Corp.

130
Institutional
Artist: **Jerry McDaniel**
Art Director: Jerry McDaniel
Client: Philip Morris International

129
Editorial
Artist: **Alan Magee**
Art Director: Joe Brooks
Publication: Penthouse Magazine

131
Book
Artist: **Harry J. Schaare**
Art Director: Harry J. Schaare

133
Film
Artist: **Len Glasser**
Art Director: Lou Dorfsman
Director: Len Glasser
Producer: Sal Butta/Colin Giles
Production: Cel Art, Inc.
Client: CBS Television Network
Gold Medal

132
Film
Artist: **Len Glasser**
Art Director: Lou Dorfsman
Director: Len Glasser
Producer: Sal Butta/Colin Giles
Production: Cel Art, Inc.
Client: CBS Television Network

134
Editorial
Artist: **John O'Leary**
Art Director: Tom Bentkowski
Publication: New York Magazine

135
Editorial
Artist: **Doug Johnson**
Art Director: Anthony Russell
Publication: Kickoff

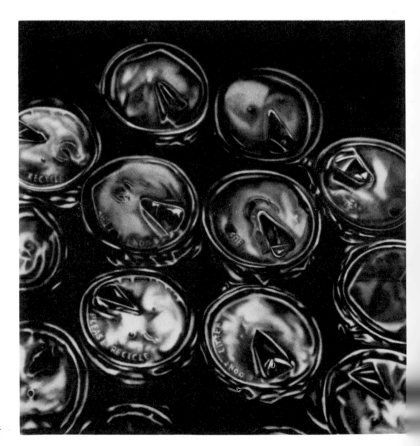

136
Institutional
Artist: **Gerald Webber**
Art Director: Gerald Webber

137
Editorial
Artist: **Joe Isom**
Art Director: Malcolm T. Young
Publication: Ford Times Magazine

138
Institutional
Artist: **John O'Leary**
Art Director: John O'Leary

139
Editorial
Artist: **David Grove**
Art Director: Gene Butera
Publication: Car and Driver Magazine

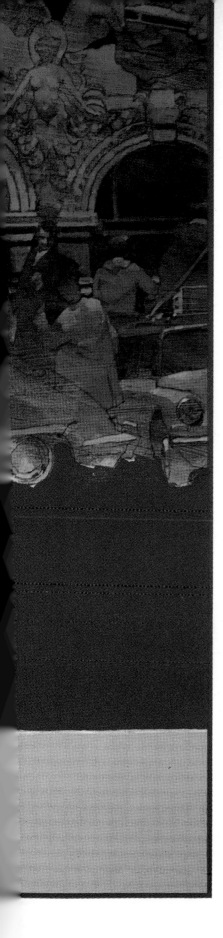

140
Editorial
Artist: **Dickran Palulian**
Art Director: Joe Brooks
Publication: Penthouse Magazine

141
Editorial
Artist: **Melinda Bordelon**
Art Director: Don Menell/Jean-Pierre Holley
Publication: Oui Magazine

142
Advertising
Artist: **Barron Storey**
Art Director: Robert Hall
Agency: Dean L. Burdick Associates, Inc.
Client: Winthrop Laboratories

143
Advertising
Artist: **Barron Storey**
Art Director: Robert Hall
Agency: Dean L. Burdick Associates, Inc.
Client: Winthrop Laboratories

144
Book
Artist: **George Ladas**
Art Director: George Ladas

145
Institutional
Artist: **Reagan Wilson**
Art Director: Reagan Wilson

146
Book
Artist: **James Spanfeller**
Art Director: Edward A. Hamilton
Title: Bank Street Series: Off Beat
Publisher: Macmillan Publishing Co., Inc.

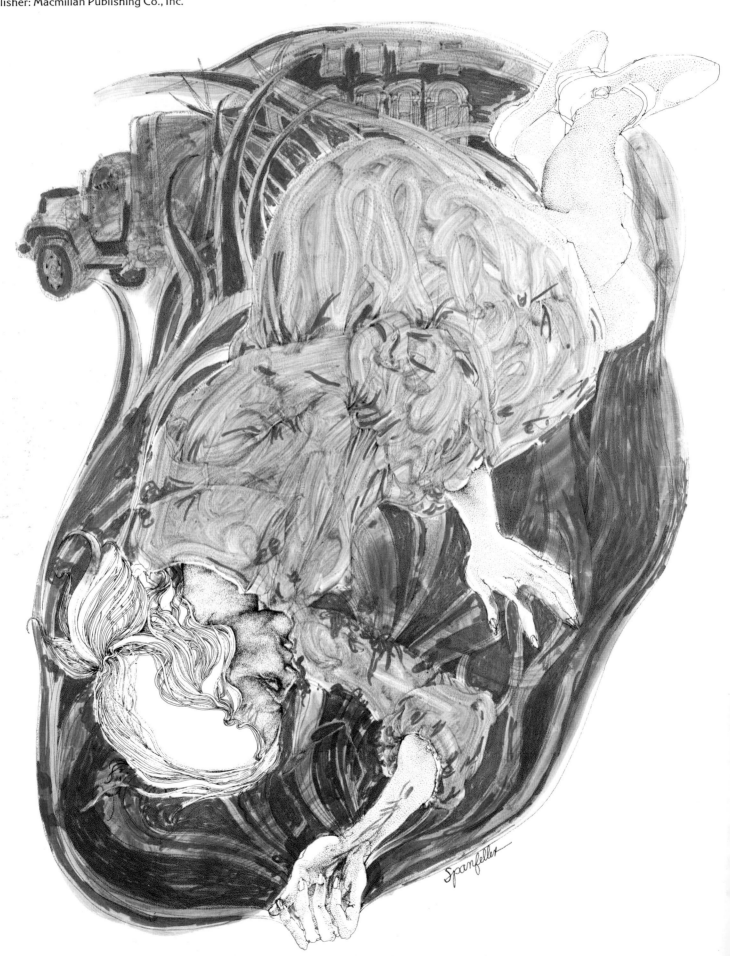

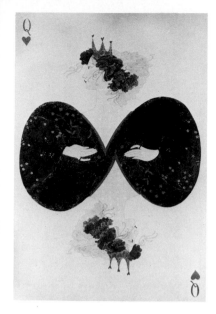

147
Institutional
Artist: **Marie Zimmerman**
Art Director: Marie Zimmerman
Agency: Neusteters
Client: Colorado Heart Association

148
Book
Artist: **Jose Aruego/Ariane Dewey**
Art Director: Riki Levinson
Title: Owliver
Publisher: Windmill Books/E. P. Dutton & Co., Inc.

149
Book
Artist: **Howard Rogers**
Art Director: Milton Charles
Title: The Handsome Road
Publisher: Pocket Books

151
Editorial
Artist: **Robert S. Lowery**
Art Director: George Cowan
Publication: The New York Times

150
Book
Artist: **Raymond Kursar**
Art Director: Richard Kapelsohn

152
Book
Artist: **Frank Frazetta**
Art Director: Bruce Hall
Title: Flashing Swords #2
Publisher: Dell Publishing Co., Inc.

153
Book
Artist: **Frank Frazetta**
Art Director: Bruce Hall
Title: The Book of Paradox
Publisher: Dell Publishing Co., Inc.

154
Book
Artist: **Howard Rogers**
Art Director: Thomas Von Der Linn
Title: Flypaper
Publisher: The Reader's Digest

155
Book
Artist: **Barbra Bergman**
Art Director: Rolf Erikson
Title: Late Call
Publisher: Curtis Books

156
Advertising
Artist: **Mark Bellerose**
Art Director: Don Kruzinski
Agency: Rumrill, Hoyt
Client: Eastman Kodak Co.

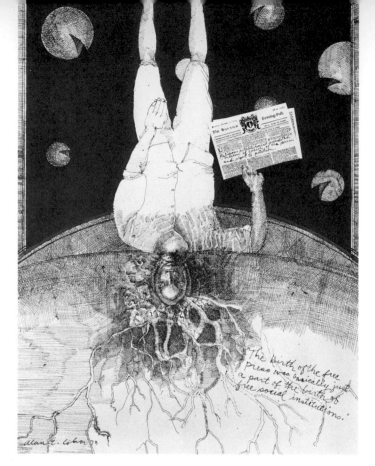

157
Book
Artist: **Alan E. Cober**
Art Director: Robert Schemmel
Title: The Rise and Falter of Free Press
Publisher: Field Enterprises Educational Corp.

158
Book
Artist: **Lorraine Fox**
Art Director: Leonard Lee Ringel
Title: Options, A Resource for
Senior Scouts
Publisher: Girl Scouts of the USA

159
Book
Artist: **Jerry Pinkney**
Art Director: Barbara Bertoli
Title: Cockleburr Quarters
Publisher: Avon Books

161
Advertising
Artist: **Bart Forbes**
Art Director: Marty Minch
Agency: Kallir, Philips, Ross, Inc.
Client: McNeil Laboratories

160
Advertising
Artist: **Barbra Bergman**
Art Director: Joseph Stelmach
Client: RCA Records

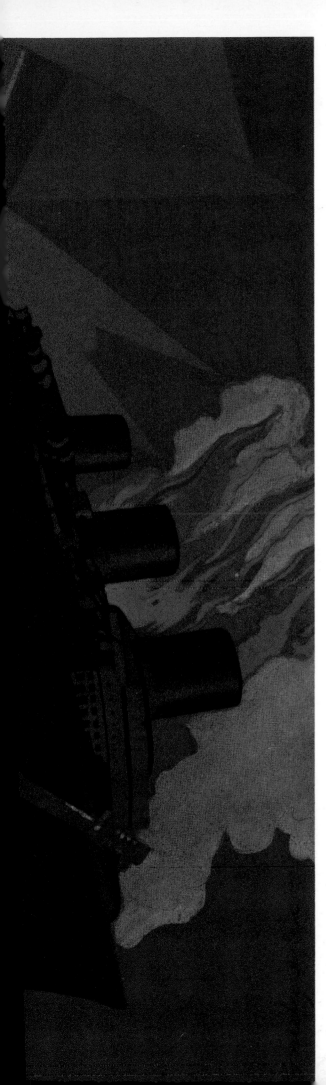

163
Institutional
Artist: **Randall McKissick**
Art Director: Bob Henderson
Agency: Henderson Design
Client: Charlotte Society of Communication Arts

162
Editorial
Artist: **Alex Gnidziejko**
Art Director: Joe Brooks
Publication: Penthouse Magazine

164
Book
Artist: **Richard Sparks**
Art Director: Richard Kapelsohn
Title: Arson and Old Lace
Publisher: Manor Books Inc.

165
Book
Artist: **Wendell Minor**
Art Director: Alex Gotfryd
Title: The Illustrated Man
Publisher: Doubleday & Co., Inc.

166
Advertising
Artist: **Reynold Ruffins**
Art Director: John Berg
Client: CBS Records

Geronimo 1886

Man asks Indian: "What was this land called before?"
Indian answers in his own language.
Man says: "What does that mean?"
Indian says: "Ours."

169
Editorial
Artist: **Barron Storey**
Art Director: Bud Loader
Publication: Flying Magazine

170
Book
Artist: **Robert Schulz**
Art Director: Milton Charles
Publisher: Pocket Books

171
Institutional
Artist: **Gary Kelley**
Art Director: Gary Kelley
Client: Hellman Design Associates, Inc.

173
Advertising
Artist: **Carol Anthony**
Art Director: Joseph Stelmach
Client: RCA Records

172
Film
Artist: **Walter Einsel**
Art Director: Walter Einsel
Photography: Warren Forma
Client: National Parks Service

174
Advertising
Artist: **Bob Peak**
Art Director: Bill Gold
Agency: Bill Gold Advertising, Inc.
Client: Warner Bros., Inc.

As Levi and Elly Zendt began their dangerous journey West, they also began their marriage. If they lacked knowledge, they had something better—youth and courage and a growing love that made them strong.

175
Editorial
Artist: **Daniel Schwartz**
Art Director: Herb Bleiweiss
Publication: Ladies' Home Journal

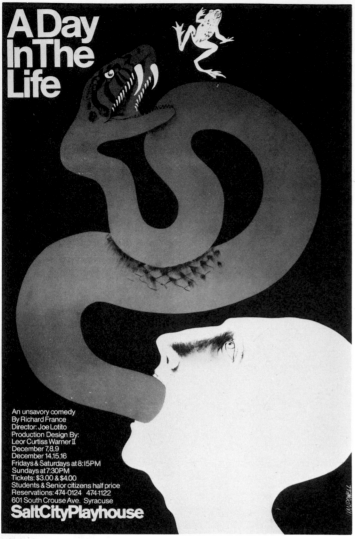

176
Advertising
Artist: **Ivan Powell**
Art Director: Ivan Powell
Agency: Mastropaul Design, Inc.
Client: Salt City Playhouse

177
Advertising
Artist: **Don Weller**
Art Director: Don Weller
Agency: The Weller Institute
Client: New York Shakespeare Festival at
    Lincoln Center

178
Advertising
Artist: **Robert S. Lowery**
Art Director: Steven R. Kidd

179
Advertising
Artist: **Ted CoConis**
Art Director: Deborah Pierce
Client: ABC Television Network

180
Advertising
Artist: **Charles White III**
Art Director: Rollin Binzer
Client: Dragon-Aire Ltd.
Gold Medal

182
Advertising
Artist: **Seymour Chwast**
Art Director: John Berg
Client: CBS Records

181
Advertising
Artist: **Alan E. Cober**
Art Director: Joseph Stelmach
Client: RCA Records

183
Book
Artist: **Peter Cross**
Art Director: Peter Cross

184
Book
Artist: **Ray Ameijide**
Art Director: Maryla Walters
Title: Do You See A Mouse
Publisher: Ginn and Company

185
Editorial
Artist: **Mark English**
Art Director: Herb Bleiweiss
Publication: Ladies' Home Journal

186
Advertising
Artist: **Raymond Kursar**
Art Director: Morris Robbins
Agency: Blaine Thompson Co., Inc.
Client: Wolsk-Azenberg

188
Book
Artist: **Murray Tinkelman**
Art Director: Ava Weiss
Title: Center of the World
Publisher: Macmillan Publishing Co., Inc.

187
Advertising
Artist: **John Collier**
Art Director: John Collier

189
Institutional
Artist: **Cliff Spohn**
Art Director: Cliff Spohn

190
Editorial
Artist: **Jean Leon Huens**
Art Director: Howard E. Paine
Publication: National Geographic Magazine

191
Advertising
Artist: **Kenneth Francis Dewey**
Art Director: Kenneth Francis Dewey
Client: Daniele Deverin

192
Book
Artist: **Ben Stahl**
Art Director: Diana Klemin
Title: Harlem
Publisher: Doubleday & Co., Inc.

193
Book
Artist: **John Ward**
Art Director: John Ward

195
Editorial
Artist: **Gilbert Stone**
Art Director: William Gregory
Publication: The Reader's Digest

Confused, agitated, and depressed, she had deteriorated to complete invalidism following brain surgery.

A case report on the management of psychotic behavior associated with organic brain syndrome.

194
Advertising
Artist: **Lorraine Fox**
Art Director: Marty Minch
Agency: Kallir, Philips, Ross, Inc.
Client: McNeil Laboratories

196
Editorial
Artist: **Wilson McLean**
Art Director: Walter Skibitsky
Publication: Scouting Magazine

197
Advertising
Artist: **Lou Myers**
Art Director: Cullen Rapp
Agency: Cullen Rapp, Inc.
Client: Cullen Rapp, Inc.

198
Editorial
Artist: **Joe Isom**
Art Director: Joe Isom
Publication: The Drovers Journal

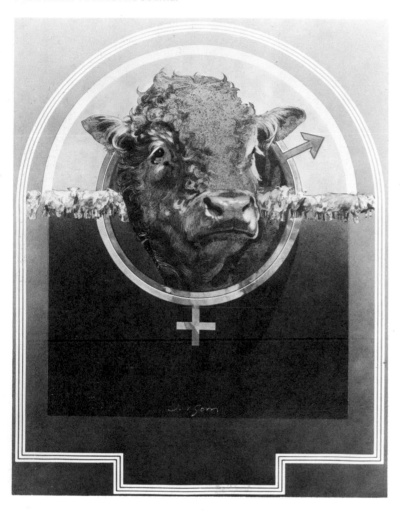

199
Book
Artist: **Karl E. Karalus**
Art Director: Diana Klemin
Title: Owls of North America
Publisher: Doubleday & Co., Inc.

200
Advertising
Artist: **Mort Kunstler**
Art Director: Martin Wolff
Agency: Wolff, Whitehill Inc.
Client: Russ Togs, Inc.

201
Editorial
Artist: **Alex Ebel**
Art Director: Don Menell/Jean-Pierre Holley
Publication: Oui Magazine

202
Institutional
Artist: **William R. Downey**
Art Director: William R. Downey

203
Book
Artist: **John Ward**
Art Director: John Ward

204
Book
Artist: **Barbara Bascove**
Art Director: Samuel N. Antupit
Title: Free to Be, You and Me
Publisher: McGraw-Hill Book Co.

205
Editorial
Artist: **John Dawson**
Art Director: Tom Gould
Publication: Psychology Today

206
Advertising
Artist: **Charles Moll**
Art Director: Wayne Salo
Agency: Diener Hauser Greenthal Co., Inc.
Client: Paramount Pictures

207
Book
Artist: **Terry L. Wickart**
Art Director: Jack O'Grady

208
Book
Artist: **Robert LoGrippo**
Art Director: Ilsa Berzins
Publisher: Macmillan Publishing Co., Inc.

209
Advertising
Artist: **Clifford Condak**
Art Director: Teresa Alfieri
Client: CBS Records

211
Advertising
Artist: **Ivan Chermayeff**
Art Director: Ivan Chermayeff
Agency: Chermayeff & Geismar Associates
Client: Mobil Oil Corp.

210
Institutional
Artist: **Hodges Soileau**
Art Director: Hodges Soileau

212
Book
Artist: **Fred Thomas**
Art Director: Fred Thomas

213
Editorial
Artist: **Robert Heindel**
Art Director: Joseph Csatari
Publication: Boys' Life Magazine

214
Film
Artist: **Alan E. Cober**
Art Director: Alan E. Cober
Client: CBS Television Network

215
Advertising
Artist: **John Collier**
Art Director: Don Scaglione
Client: Arton Associates, Inc.
Gold Medal

216
Advertising
Artist: **Stanislaw Zagorski**
Art Director: Bob Defrin
Client: Atlantic Records

217
Editorial
Artist: **Bruce Emmett**
Art Director: Bruce Emmett

218
Advertising
Artist: **D.R. Shuck**
Art Director: D.R. Shuck
Client: The Wire Wheel

220
Advertising
Artist: **Richard Harvey**
Art Director: Neil Terk
Client: Chess Janis Records

219
Editorial
Artist: **Bob Walker**
Art Director: Victoria Romaine
Publication: Scope Magazine

221
Advertising
Artist: **Bob Radigan**
Art Director: Bob Radigan

222
Advertising
Artist: **Phil Carroll**
Art Director: Tony Lane
Client: Fantasy Records

223
Advertising
Artist: **Roger Hane**
Art Director: John Berg
Client: CBS Records
Award for Excellence

224
Book
Artist: **Steve Karchin**
Art Director: Gerry Contreras

225
Book
Artist: **Gerald McConnell**
Art Director: Milton Charles
Title: Shocking Thing
Publisher: Pocket Books

226
Editorial
Artist: **John Collier**
Art Director: William F. Cadge
Publication: Redbook

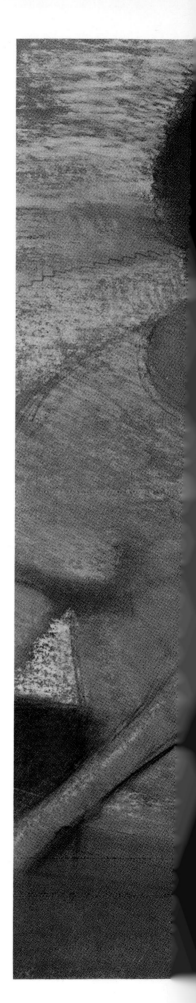

228
Editorial
Artist: **Barbara Nessim**
Art Director: Ahmad Sadiq
Publication: Viva Magazine

227
Institutional
Artist: **Siegbert Reinhard**
Art Director: Siegbert Reinhard
Client: Cullen Rapp, Inc.

229
Book
Artist: **Ted CoConis**
Art Director: Bill Gregory
Title: Harlequin
Publisher: The Reader's Digest

230
Editorial
Artist: **Daniel Maffia**
Art Director: Ahmad Sadiq
Publication: Viva Magazine

231
Editorial
Artist: **Philip Fazio**
Art Director: Philip Fazio

234
Editorial
Artist: **Richard Bober**
Art Director: Linda Cox
Publication: Cosmopolitan

233
Advertising
Artist: **Vin Giuliani**
Art Director: Dick Nathan
Client: Elaine Sorel

232
Advertising
Artist: **Bill Imhoff**
Art Director: Beverly Parker/Ron Coro
Client: Columbia Records

235
Editorial
Artist: **Doug Gervasi**
Art Director: Art Kane/Roy Carruthers
Publication: Viva Magazine

236
Editorial
Artist: **Bill Buerge**
Art Director: Tom Gould
Publication: Psychology Today

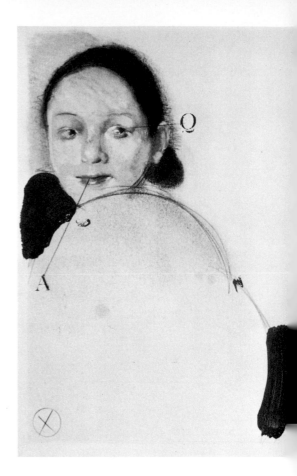

237
Editorial
Artist: **Robert M. Cunningham**
Art Director: B. Martin Pedersen
Publication: Pastimes Magazine

238
Editorial
Artist: **Daniel Schwartz**
Art Director: William Gregory
Publication: The Reader's Digest

239
Editorial
Artist: **John Collier**
Art Director: John Collier
Award for Excellence

240
Editorial
Artist: **Bob Newman**
Art Director: Cliff Gardiner
Publication: LI Magazine

241
Advertising
Artist: **Oni**
Art Director: Oni

243
Editorial
Artist: **Bart Forbes**
Art Director: Modesto Torre
Publication: McCall's Magazine

242
Editorial
Artist: **Steve Karchin**
Art Director: Gerry Contreras

244
Editorial
Artist: **Paul Giovanopoulos**
Art Director: Paul Giovanopoulos

245
Editorial
Artist: **Carol Wald**
Art Director: Art Kane
Publication: Viva Magazine
Gold Medal

246
Book
Artist: **Richard Harvey**
Art Director: Thomas Von Der Linn
Title: From Russia, With Love
Publisher: The Reader's Digest

247
Book
Artist: **Robert Tallon**
Art Director: Robert Tallon

248
Advertising
Artist: **Dorothy Wozniak**
Art Director: Larry Pillot
Agency: Lang, Fisher & Stashower
Client: Cleveland Trust

249
Editorial
Artist: **Christian Piper**
Art Director: Art Kane
Publication: Viva Magazine

251
Editorial
Artist: **Ted CoConis**
Art Director: Kristen Schleicher
Publication: Cosmopolitan

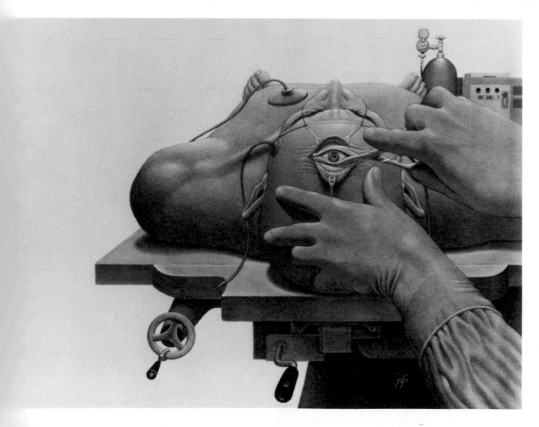

250
Editorial
Artist: **Don Ivan Punchatz**
Art Director: Arthur Paul
Publication: Playboy Magazine

252
Editorial
Artist: **Carol Wald**
Art Director: Art Kane
Publication: Viva Magazine

253
Editorial
Artist: **George Jones**
Art Director: Marion Davis
Publication: The Reader's Digest

254
Advertising
Artist: **Howard Rogers**
Art Director: Marty Minch
Agency: Kallir, Philips, Ross Inc.
Client: McNeil Laboratories

255
Book
Artist: **John Berkey**
Art Director: Bruce Hall
Title: Deep Space
Publisher: Dell Publishing Co., Inc.

256
Advertising
Artist: **John Berkey**
Art Director: Larry Wattman/Jerry Leopold
Agency: Poppe-Tyson Inc.
Client: Otis Elevator Co.

257
Editorial
Artist: **David Blossom**
Art Director: Marion Davis
Publication: The Reader's Digest

259
Book
Artist: **Robert Schulz**
Art Director: Milton Charles
Publisher: Pocket Books

258
Book
Artist: **David Macaulay**
Art Director: Walter Lorraine
Title: City
Publisher: Houghton Mifflin Co.

262
Advertising
Artist: **Elwyn Mehlman**
Art Director: Larry Pillot
Agency: Lang, Fisher & Stashower
Client: Cleveland Trust

261
Institutional
Artist: **Ray Domingo**
Art Director: Ray Domingo
Agency: E&R Graphics
Client: Cooper School of Art

263
Editorial
Artist: **Chuck Wilkinson**
Art Director: Chuck Wilkinson

260
Institutional
Artist: **Jerry Harston**
Art Director: Preston Heiselt
Agency: LDS Graphic Design Dept.
Client: Promised Valley Playhouse

264
Institutional
Artist: **Jared D. Lee**
Art Director: Anne Sellers Leaf
Client: Gibson Greeting Cards

265
Advertising
Artist: **Jerry Cosgrove**
Art Director: Ace Lehman
Client: RCA Records

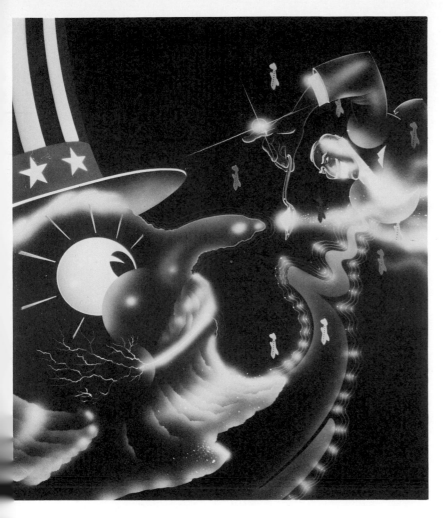

266
Editorial
Artist: **Peter Lloyd**
Art Director: Don Menell/George Kenton
Publication: Oui Magazine
Award for Excellence

267
Advertising
Artist: **Charles Santore**
Art Director: Jeff Odiorn
Agency: N. W. Ayer & Son, Inc.
Client: TV Guide

268
Advertising
Artist: **Bill Chambers**
Art Director: Bill Harkins
Agency: Grant Jacoby Inc.
Client: Caterpillar Tractor Co.

269
Advertising
Artist: **Howard Rogers**
Art Director: William Vogt
Agency: J. Walter Thompson Co.
Client: Eli Lilly & Co.

270
Editorial
Artist: **Don Ivan Punchatz**
Art Director: Michael Gross
Publication: National Lampoon
Award for Excellence

271
Institutional
Artist: **Andrew Nawrocky**
Art Director: Mike Palombo
Agency: Norman Affiliates Ltd.
Client: Hoffmann-La Roche, Inc.

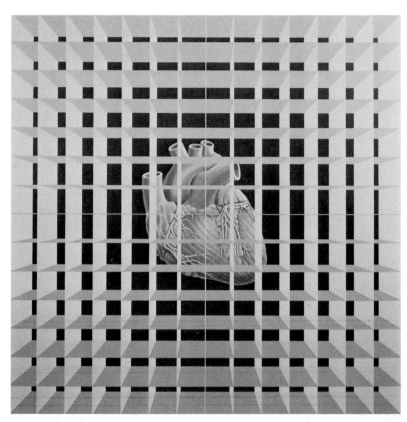

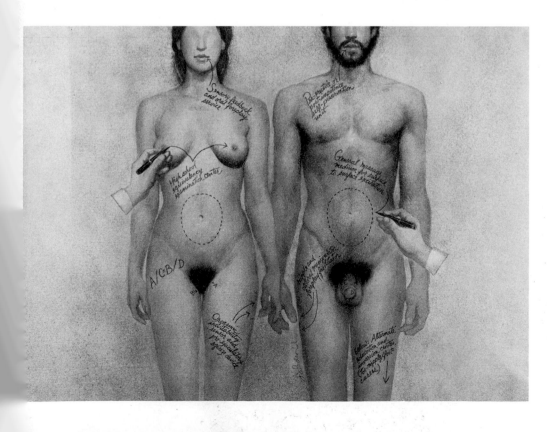

272
Editorial
Artist: **Jerome Podwil**
Art Director: Art Paul
Publication: Playboy Magazine

274
Advertising
Artist: **John O'Leary**
Art Director: John W. Channell
Agency: Group One Creative Graphics, Inc.
Client: Sony Corporation of America

273
Book
Artist: **Paul Bacon**
Art Director: R. D. Scudellari
Title: Frankenstein Unbound
Publisher: Random House, Inc.

275
Editorial
Artist: **Simms Taback**
Art Director: Charles Curtis
Publication: World Magazine

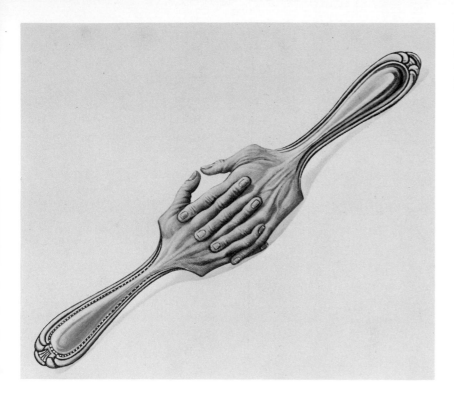

276
Advertising
Artist: **Richard Hess**
Art Director: Mike Lyons
Agency: Sudler & Hennessey, Inc.
Client: Pfizer International

278
Advertising
Artist: **Barry Ross**
Art Director: Warren McLoad
Agency: Wessen & Warharftig
Client: Ayerst Laboratories

277
Advertising
Artist: **Gervaslo Gallardo**
Art Director: Anthony V. Leone
Agency: Lewis & Gilman, Advertising Inc.
Client: Roerig/Division of Pfizer Laboratories

279
Advertising
Artist: **Milton Glaser**
Art Director: John Berg
Client: CBS Records

280
Advertising
Artist: **Dave Wilcox**
Art Director: Edwin E. Lee
Client: CBS Records

281
Advertising
Artist: **Don Brautigam**
Art Director: Paula Bisacca
Client: Atlantic Records

282
Advertising
Artist: **Barry Smith**
Art Director: John Berg
Client: CBS Records

283
Advertising
Artist: **Phil Carroll**
Art Director: Tony Lane
Client: Prestige Records

285
Editorial
Artist: **James McMullan**
Art Director: Walter Bernard
Publication: New York Magazine

284
Book
Artist: **James McMullan**
Art Director: Ian Summers
Title: The Persecutor
Publisher: Ballantine Books, Inc.

286
Book
Artist: **Donald M. Hedin**
Art Director: Bruce Hall
Title: Recipes for Beautiful Soup
Publisher: Dell Publishing Co., Inc.

287
Editorial
Artist: **Stanley Meltzoff**
Art Director: Richard Gangel
Publication: Sports Illustrated

288
Editorial
Artist: **Don Ivan Punchatz**
Art Director: Don Menell/Jean-Pierre Holley
Publication: Oui Magazine

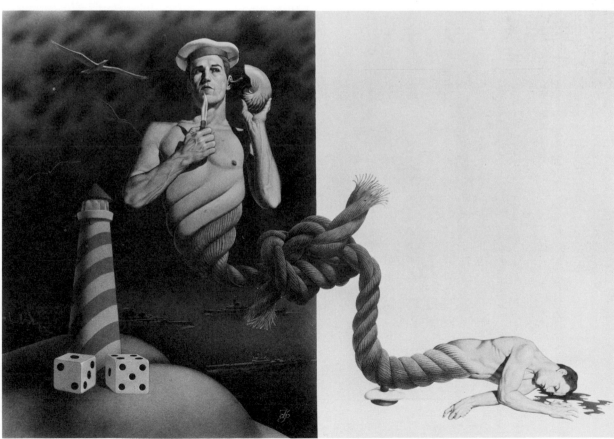

289
Editorial
Artist: **Mark Stamaty**
Art Director: Richard Weiland
Publication: Esquire Magazine

290
Advertising
Artist: **Joe Shyllit**
Art Director: Joe Shyllit
Agency: Goodis, Goldberg, Soren

291
Advertising
Artist: **Theo Rudnak**
Art Director: Larry Pillot
Agency: Lang, Fisher & Stashower
Client: Cleveland Trust

292
Editorial
Artist: **Terry Steadham**
Art Director: Lawrence Simmons
Publication: Child Life Magazine

295
Editorial
Artist: **David A. Johnson**
Art Director: Ira Silberlicht/Tom Lennon
Publication: Emergency Medicine

293
Book
Artist: **George Guzzi**
Art Director: George Guzzi

294
Book
Artist: **Judith Jampel**
Art Director: Judith Jampel

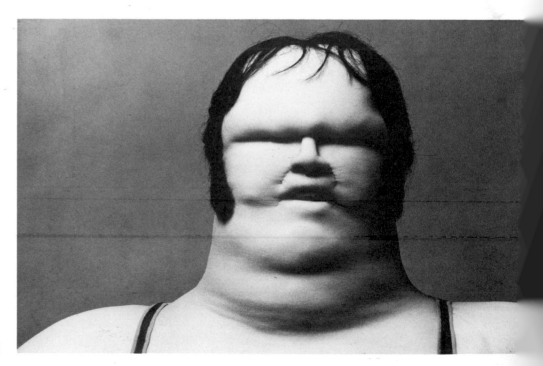

296
Advertising
Artist: **Stan Hunter**
Art Director: Marty Minch
Agency: Kallir, Philips, Ross Inc.
Client: McNeil Laboratories

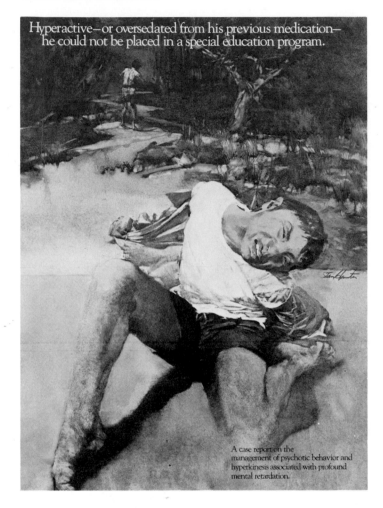

297
Advertising
Artist: **Arnold Varga**
Art Director: Clem Cykowski
Agency: Campbell-Ewald Co., Inc.
Client: Chevrolet Motor Division—General Motors Corp.

298
Editorial
Artist: **Don Ivan Punchatz**
Art Director: Arthur Paul
Publication: Playboy Magazine

301
Editorial
Artist: **Don Weller**
Art Director: Elin Waite
Publication: Westways Magazine

299
Book
Artist: **Jim Sharpe**
Art Director: William Gregory
Title: The Good Shepherd
Publisher: The Reader's Digest

300
Institutional
Artist: **Steven Carter**
Art Director: William Tinker
Client: Hallmark Cards

MAY 1974

WESTWAYS

Welter

302
Book
Artist: **Robert Byrd**
Art Director: Robert Kraus/Riki Levinson
Title: Pinchpenny Mouse
Publisher: Windmill Books/E.P. Dutton & Co., Inc.

303
Editorial
Artist: **Seymour Chwast**
Art Director: Henry Wolf
Publication: Sesame St. Magazine

305
Book
Artist: **Kay Chorao**
Art Director: Riki Levinson
Title: Albert's Toothache
Publisher: E. P. Dutton & Co., Inc.

304
Advertising
Artist: **Robert C. Kinyon**
Art Director: Robert Perine
Agency: Frye & Smith Ltd.
Client: San Diego Zoo

306
Book
Artist: **Diane Martin**
Art Director: Carol Bancroft

307
Book
Artist: **Nicholas Gaetano**
Art Director: Catherine Hopkins
Title: Mark Twain
Publisher: Harper & Row, Publishers, Inc.

308
Book
Artist: **Jack Endewelt**
Art Director: Bruce Hall
Title: A Wind in the Door
Publisher: Dell Publishing Co., Inc.

309
Editorial
Artist: **Alex Gnidziejko**
Art Director: Don Menell
Publication: Oui Magazine

312
Editorial
Artist: **Joe Isom**
Art Director: Joseph Csatari
Publication: Boys' Life Magazine

310
Editorial
Artist: **David Wilcox**
Art Director: Don Menell/Michael Brock
Publication: Oui Magazine

311
Book
Artist: **Gervasio Gallardo**
Art Director: Bob Blanchard
Title: Double Phoenix
Publisher: Ballantine Books, Inc.

313
Advertising
Artist: **Tom Daly**
Art Director: John Cenatiempo
Agency: Gaynor-Ducas Advertising
Client: Union-Camp

314
Book
Artist: **Gerald McConnell**
Art Director: Susan Phillips
Title: American History
Publisher: Alfred A. Knopf, Inc.

315
Book
Artist: **Marvin Goldman/Marilyn Bass**
Art Director: Dhyana Hollingsworth
Title: The Americans
Publisher: Holt, Rinehart and Winston, Inc.

Holt
nehart
inston

317
Editorial
Artist: **Miriam Wosk**
Art Director: Art Kane
Publication: Viva Magazine

316
Editorial
Artist: **Nicholas Gaetano**
Art Director: Dave Phillips
Publication: New Times Magazine

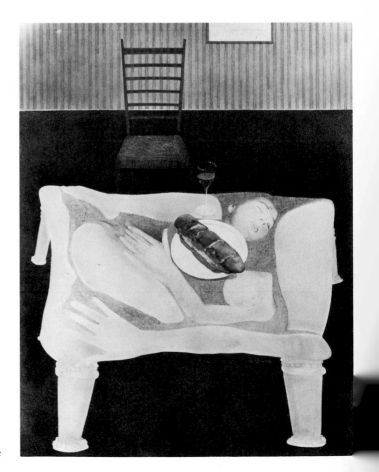

318
Editorial
Artist: **Robert Heindel**
Art Director: Ahmad Sadiq
Publication: Viva Magazine

This is the farmer sowing his corn,
That kept the cock that crowed in the morn,
That waked the priest all shaven and shorn,
That married the man all tattered and torn,
That kissed the maiden all forlorn,
That milked the cow with the crumpled horn,
That tossed the dog,
That worried the cat,
That killed the rat,
That ate the malt
That lay in the house
that Jack built.

319
Book
Artist: **Seymour Chwast**
Art Director: Eleanor Ehrhardt
Title: The House That Jack Built
Publisher: Random House, Inc.

320
Book
Artist: **Cliff Condak**
Art Director: Louis Fulgoni
Title: The Brinks Caper
Publisher: The Stonehouse Press
Award for Excellence

322
Book
Artist: **Dennis Luczak**
Art Director: Dennis Luczak

321
Editorial
Artist: **Sketch Pad Studio**
Art Director: Don Menell/Jean-Pierre Holley
Publication: Oui Magazine

323
Advertising
Artist: **Richard J. Behm**
Art Director: Richard J. Behm
Agency: Lord, Sullivan & Yoder Advertising
Client: Lord, Sullivan & Yoder Advertising

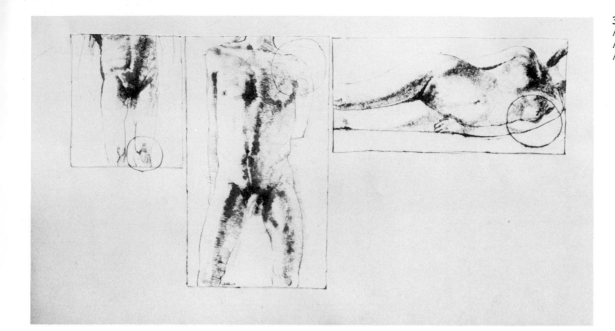

324
Advertising
Artist: **John Collier**
Art Director: John Collier

326
Editorial
Artist: **Carol Wald**
Art Director: Carl Barke
Publication: Viva Magazine

325
Editorial
Artist: **Richard Sparks**
Art Director: Joseph Connolly
Publication: Genesis Magazine

327
Book
Artist: **George Guzzi**
Art Director: George Guzzi

328
Editorial
Artist: **Jerry Podwil**
Art Director: Arthur Paul
Publication: Playboy Magazine

329
Advertising
Artist: **Carol Anthony**
Art Director: Andrew Kner
Client: The New York Times

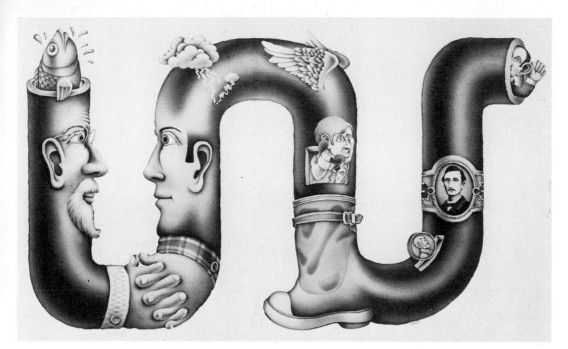

334
Advertising
Artist: **Elwyn Mehlman**
Art Director: Petter Thoen
Agency: Griswold-Eshelman
Client: B. F. Goodrich

335
Advertising
Artist: **Gary Solin**
Art Director: Andrew Kner
Client: The New York Times

333
Editorial
Artist: **Ronald Searle**
Art Director: Norman S. Hotz
Publication: Travel & Leisure Magazine

336
Editorial
Artist: **Seymour Chwast**
Art Director: Ruth Ansel
Publication: The New York Times

337
Editorial
Artist: **Edward Sorel**
Art Director: Ruth Ansel
Publication: The New York Times

338
Institutional
Artist: **Carol Wald**
Art Director: Carol Wald

339
Advertising
Artist: **Richard Harvey**
Art Director: Richard Harvey

340
Editorial
Artist: **Jane Sterrett**
Art Director: Jane Sterrett

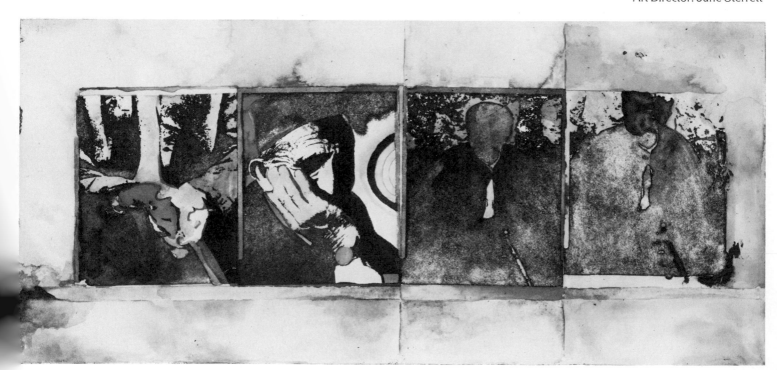

EMERGENCY
MEDICINE

MAY 1974

341
Editorial
Artist: **Frank Bozzo**
Art Director: Ira Silberlicht/Tom Lennon
Publication: Emergency Medicine

342
Editorial
Artist: **Pierre Le-Tan**
Art Director: Robert Essman
Publication: Business Week Magazine

343
Advertising
Artist: **Mark English**
Art Director: Frank Wagner
Agency: Sudler & Hennessey, Inc.
Client: Pfizer Laboratories

345
Book
Artist: **Darrell Sweet**
Art Director: Marion Davis
Title: Forever Island
Publisher: The Reader's Digest

344
Institutional
Artist: **Alan E. Cober**
Art Director: Bill Duevell/Diana Graham/Alan E. Cober
Client: Holt Children's Fund

346
Institutional
Artist: **Tom Fish**
Art Director: Sharon Stolzenberger
Client: Gibson Greeting Cards

347
Book
Artist: **Martin Lemelman**
Art Director: Martin Lemelman

348
Editorial
Artist: **Robert Weaver**
Art Director: Richard Gangel
Publication: Sports Illustrated

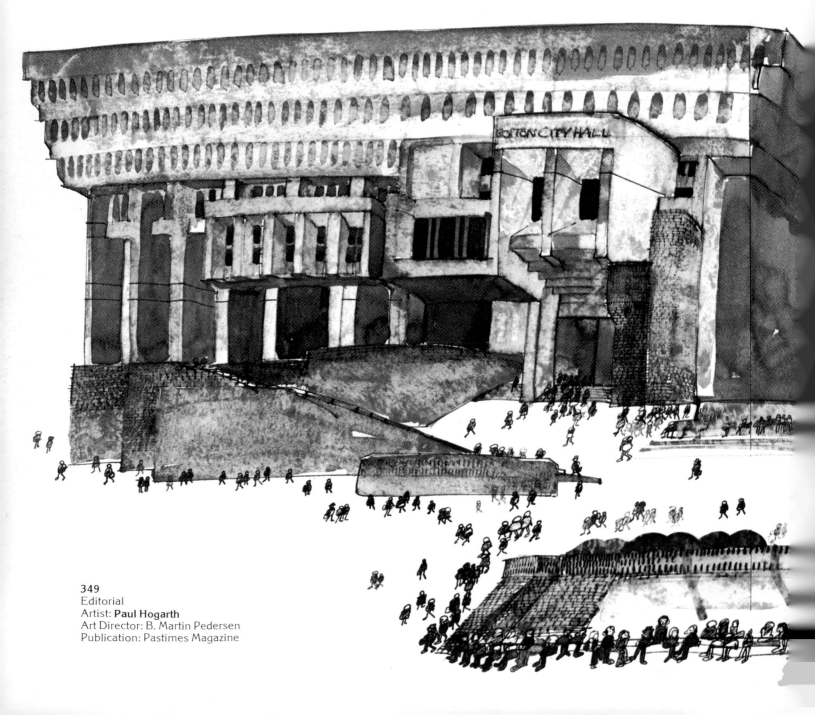

349
Editorial
Artist: **Paul Hogarth**
Art Director: B. Martin Pedersen
Publication: Pastimes Magazine

350
Advertising
Artist: **Denise Saldutti**
Art Director: Lorraine Fox/Denis Orloff

351
Institutional
Artist: **Norman MacDonald**
Art Director: Miranda & Kenneth Hine

352
Book
Artist: **John Cayea**
Art Director: Rallou Hamshaw
Title: House of Zeor
Publisher: Doubleday & Co., Inc.

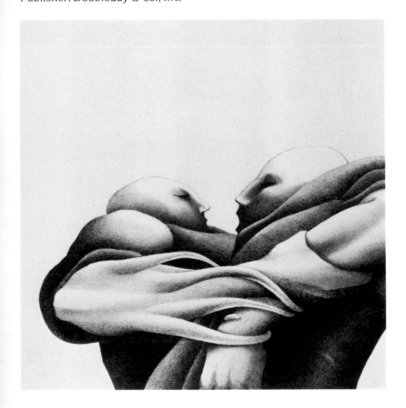

353
Book
Artist: **Jeffrey Cornell**
Art Director: Ian Summers
Title: Deltoid Pumpkin Seed
Publisher: Ballantine Books, Inc.

354
Editorial
Artist: **Alex Gnidziejko**
Art Director: Don Menell
Publication: Oui Magazine

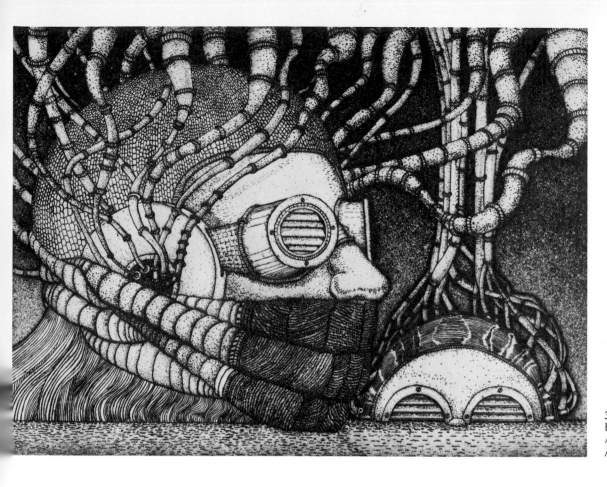

355
Editorial
Artist: **Christopher J. Spollen**
Art Director: Christopher J. Spollen

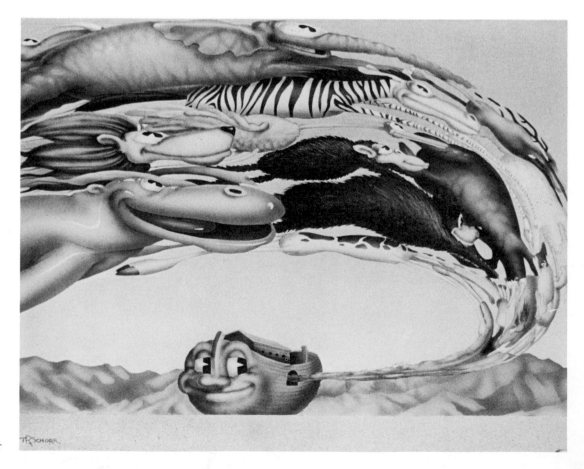

356
Book
Artist: **Todd Schorr**
Art Director: Todd Schorr

357
Institutional
Artist: **John O'Leary**
Art Director: John W. Channell
Agency: Group One Creative Graphics, Inc.
Client: Sony Corporation of America
Award for Excellence

358
Institutional
Artist: **Glenn Bradshaw**
Art Director: A. A. Versh
Client: American Artists Group, Inc.

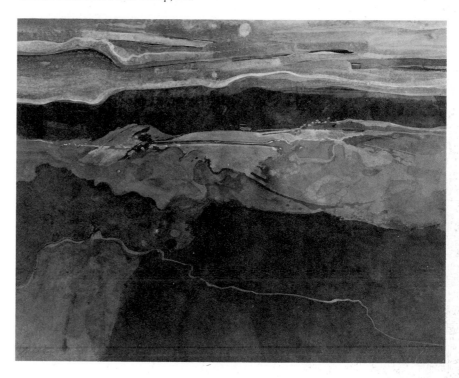

359
Advertising
Artist: **Dorothy Kegel**
Art Director: Sandra Rigney
Agency: Donýa Melanson Associates

360
Editorial
Artist: **George Sottung**
Art Director: George Sottung

362
Editorial
Artist: **J. Daniel Chapman**
Art Director: Wanda Coleman
Publication: Players Magazine

361
Institutional
Artist: **Paul G. Melia**
Art Director: Dan Johnson
Client: Pflaum Publishing

363
Book
Artist: **Wendell Minor**
Art Director: Alex Gotfryd
Title: Wait Until Evening
Publisher: Doubleday & Co., Inc.

364
Institutional
Artist: **Alan E. Cober**
Art Director: Nick Kirilloff
Client: National Parks Service
Award for Excellence

365
Editorial
Artist: **John Ward**
Art Director: John Ward

366
Book
Artist: **David Palladini**
Art Director: Sallie Baldwin
Title: The End of the World
Publisher: Thomas Y. Crowell Co.

367
Advertising
Artist: **John Keely**
Art Director: John Keely

368
Book
Artist: **Darrell Sweet**
Art Director: Ian Summers
Title: The Long Tomorrow
Publisher: Ballantine Books, Inc.

369
Film
Artist: **Bob Kurtz**
Art Director: John Sapienza
Agency: Van Brunt & Co.
Client: New England Fish Co.
Award for Excellence

370
Film
Artist: **Phil Smith**
Art Director: Howard Imhoff
Agency: Doremus & Co.
Client: Dime Savings Bank of New York

371
Advertising
Artist: **Ted CoConis**
Art Director: Deborah Pierce
Client: Jim Henson, Inc.

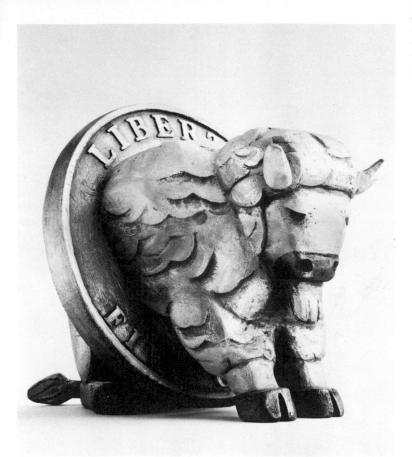

372
Advertising
Artist: **Elaine Wozniak**
Art Director: Larry Pillot
Agency: Lang, Fisher & Stashower
Client: Cleveland Trust

374
Film
Artist: **R. O. Blechman**
Art Director: Rod Capawana
Agency: Doremus & Co.
Client: National Association of Insurance Agents

373
Advertising
Artist: **Ed Geiger**
Art Director: Bill Alderisio
Agency: J. Walter Thompson Co.
Client: Parke Davis, Canada

375
Editorial
Artist: **Vin Giuliani**
Art Director: Philip Dykstra
Publication: Modern Medicine

376
Editorial
Artist: **Dickran Palulian**
Art Director: Dickran Palulian

377
Advertising
Artist: **Peter Palombi**
Art Director: Basil Pao
Client: Atlantic Records

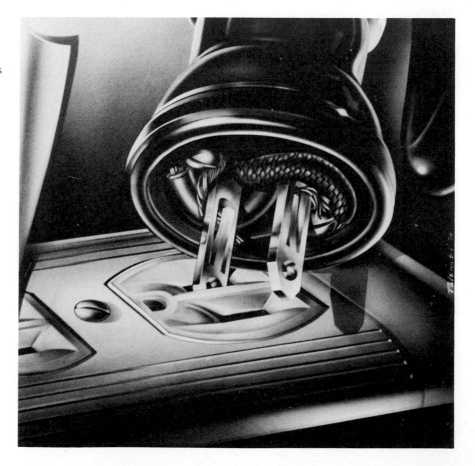

379
Advertising
Artist: **David Palladini**
Art Director: David Palladini
Client: Jane Lander Associates

378
Book
Artist: **David Passalacqua**
Art Director: Leonard P. Leone
Title: A Thousand Summers
Publisher: Bantam Books, Inc.

380
Editorial
Artist: **Carol Bouman**
Art Director: Michael Brock
Publication: Oui Magazine

381
Advertising
Artist: **Dennis Pohl**
Art Director: Dennis Pohl
Client: Jane Lander Associates

382
Advertising
Artist: **Bob Pepper**
Art Director: Carl Anderson
Agency: Essie Pinsker Associates, Inc.
Client: Cranston Print Works Co.

383
Editorial
Artist: **Jack N. Unruh**
Art Director: Frederick Schneider
Publication: Crawdaddy Magazine

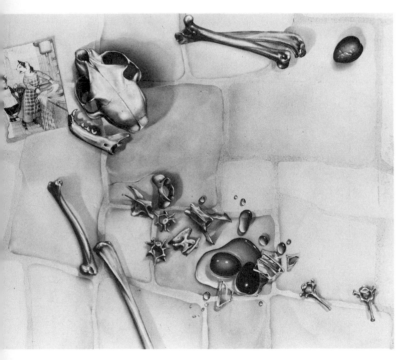

384
Editorial
Artist: **Charles White III**
Art Director: Don Menell/Jean-Pierre Holley
Publication: Oui Magazine

385
Book
Artist: **Barbra Bergman**
Art Director: Rolf Erikson
Title: Anglo Saxon Attitudes
Publisher: Curtis Books

386
Book
Artist: **Don Ivan Punchatz**
Art Director: John Van Zwienen
Title: Mother Night
Publisher: Dell Publishing Co., Inc.

387
Book
Artist: **Don Ivan Punchatz**
Art Director: James Plumeri
Title: Night's Yawning Peal
Publisher: New American Library

388
Book
Artist: **Ken Rinciari**
Art Director: Zlata Paces
Title: Why
Publisher: Macmillan Publishing Co., Inc.

389
Editorial
Artist: **Holland S. Macdonald**
Art Director: Holland S. Macdonald

390
Book
Artist: **Lucinda McQueen**
Art Director: Will Winslow
Title: The Cake Story
Publisher: Addison-Wesley Publishing Co., Inc.

391
Advertising
Artist: **Birney Lettick**
Art Director: Dick Knipe
Agency: Bill Gold Advertising, Inc.
Client: Columbia Pictures

392
Editorial
Artist: **Patrick Byrne**
Art Director: Don Menell/George Kenton
Publication: Oui Magazine

394
Advertising
Artist: **Gerry Gersten**
Art Director: Frank Atardi
Agency: Atardi, Nogid, Watnik
Client: E. B. Meyrowitz, Inc.

393
Book
Artist: **Jack Endewelt**
Art Director: Ken Sneider/Nick Calabrese
Title: Padre Ulivo and His Friends
Publisher: The Reader's Digest

395
Editorial
Artist: **Sandy Huffaker**
Art Director: Dick Boland
Publication: National Observer

396
Advertising
Artist: **Raymond Ameijide**
Art Director: Henry Epstein
Client: American Broadcasting Companies, Inc.

397
Advertising
Artist: **Dennis Ziemienski**
Art Director: Steve Jacobs
Agency: Steve Jacobs Design
Client: Simpson Lee Paper Co.

398
Book
Artist: **Byron Barton**
Art Director: Ava Weiss
Title: Harry is a Scaredy-Cat
Publisher: Macmillan Publishing Co., Inc.

399
Advertising
Artist: **Charles Santore**
Art Director: Anthony V. Leone
Agency: Lewis & Gilman, Inc.
Client: Roerig/Division of Pfizer Laboratories

400
Advertising
Artist: **David Plourde**
Art Director: Len Obsatz
Agency: Sudler & Hennessey, Inc.
Client: Roerig/Pfizer Laboratories

401
Book
Artist: **Allen Davis**
Art Director: Allen Davis

402
Institutional
Artist: **Nancy Lee Ohanian**
Art Director: Nancy Lee Ohanian

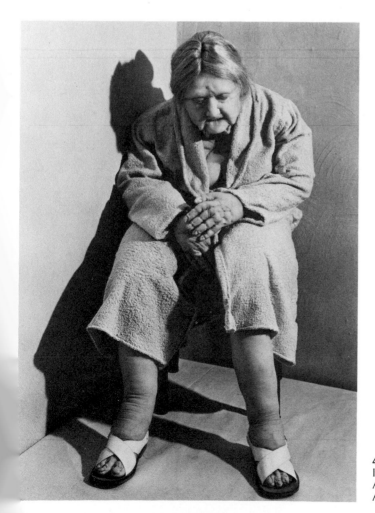

404
Book
Artist: **John C. Wallner**
Art Director: Alexandra Czesnykowski

403
Institutional
Artist: **Judith Jampel**
Art Director: Judith Jampel

405
Advertising
Artist: **Nick Aristovulos**
Art Director: Bob Defrin
Client: Manticore Records

406
Book
Artist: **Tom Hall**
Art Director: Barbara Bertoli
Title: The Moneyman
Publisher: Avon Books

407
Book
Artist: **Robert LoGrippo**
Art Director: Ilsa Bersons
Title: Unicorns
Publisher: Macmillan Publishing Co., Inc.

408
Book
Artist: **William S. Shields**
Art Director: Edward A. Hamilton
Title: The English Tradition: Drama
Publisher: Macmillan Publishing Co., Inc.
Award for Excellence

409
Book
Artist: **Paul Williams**
Art Director: Paul Williams

410
Book
Artist: **Mark Livingston**
Art Director: Betty Anderson
Title: An Everyday History of Somewhere
Publisher: Random House, Inc.

411
Editorial
Artist: **Max Gottfried**
Art Director: Max Gottfried

412
Book
Artist: **Joel Schick**
Art Director: Jean Krulis
Title: The Gobble'uns Will Get You
      If You Don't Watch Out
Publisher: J. B. Lippincott Co.

413
Advertising
Artist: **Marshall Arisman**
Art Director: Richard Wilde
Client: School of Visual Arts

414
Advertising
Artist: **Everett Davidson**
Art Director: Everett Davidson

415
Advertising
Artist: **Lewis McCance**
Art Director: Carl Herrman
Client: The Literary Guild

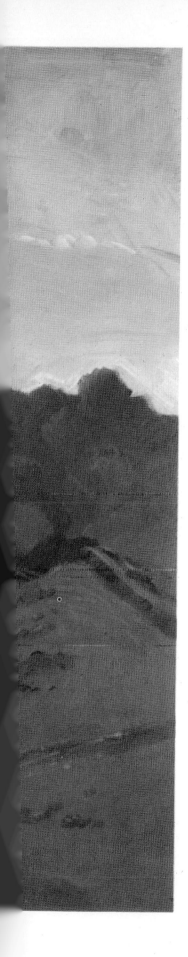

416
Editorial
Artist: **Steve Karchin**
Art Director: Gerry Contreras

417
Advertising
Artist: **Robert Andrew Parker**
Art Director: Henrietta Condak
Client: CBS Records

418
Advertising
Artist: **Helmut K. Wimmer**
Art Director: Teresa Alfieri
Client: CBS Records

419
Book
Artist: **David Palladini**
Art Director: Sallie Baldwin
Title: The End of the World
Publisher: Thomas Y. Crowell Co.

420
Editorial
Artist: **Clint Crosthwaite**
Art Director: Clint Crosthwaite

In the early days of mail delivery, local butchers frequently saw to it that posted letters reached their destination. Considering the times, butchers made fairly efficient postmen, since they had a fixed schedule of slaughtering rounds that brought them into routine contact with almost every local resident.

421
Institutional
Artist: **Chris Duke**
Art Director: Eric Rathje
Agency: Dugan/Farley Communication
Client: Clark-O'Neill, Inc.

422
Book
Artist: **Nita Engle**
Art Director: Marion Davis
Title: The Mountain Farm
Publisher: The Reader's Digest

423
Advertising
Artist: **Cliff Spohn**
Art Director: Bob Murray
Client: Memorex

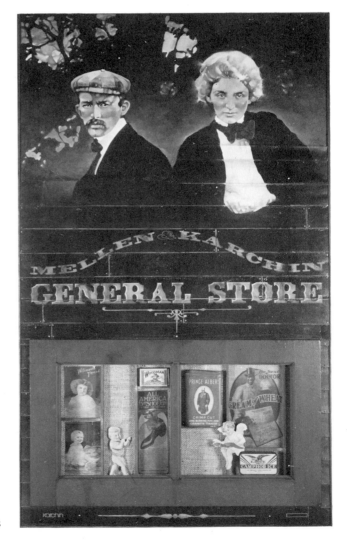

425
Institutional
Artist: **Steve Karchin**
Art Director: Gerry Contreras

424
Editorial
Artist: **Dennis Luczak**
Art Director: Dennis Luczak

426
Editorial
Artist: **Liam Roberts**
Art Director: Tom Ries
Publication: American Way

427
Editorial
Artist: **Graham McCallum**
Art Director: Joe Brooks
Publication: Penthouse Magazine

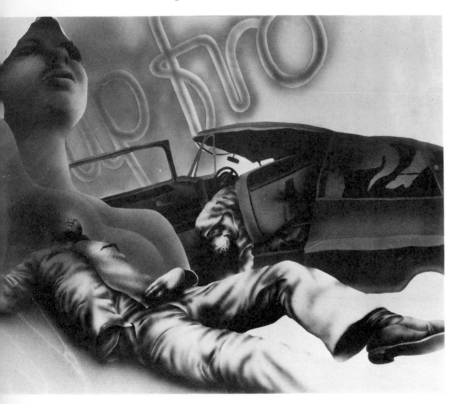

428
Advertising
Artist: **Wilson McLean**
Art Director: Dolores Gudzin
Client: NBC-TV

429
Editorial
Artist: **Keith Lesselyoung**
Art Director: Keith Lesselyoung

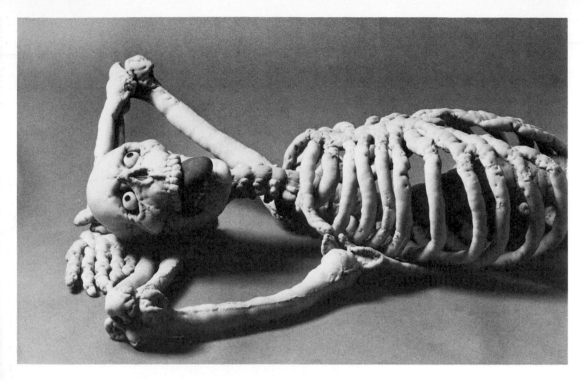

430
Advertising
Artist: **Judith Jampel**
Art Director: Judith Jampel

431
Editorial
Artist: **William S. Shields**
Art Director: Ira Silberlicht/Tom Lennon
Publication: Emergency Medicine

432
Book
Artist: **Robert Grossman**
Art Director: Ian Summers
Title: The Mad Reader
Publisher: Ballantine Books, Inc.

433
Book
Artist: **Judy Pelikan**
Art Director: Steve Snider

434
Editorial
Artist: **William Accorsi**
Art Director: Skip Sorvino
Publication: Scholastic Magazine

435
Editorial
Artist: **Nancy Freeman**
Art Director: Bill Buerge
Publication: Southland Sunday

436
Advertising
Artist: **Edward Sorel**
Art Director: John Berg
Client: CBS Records

437
Advertising
Artist: **Christian Piper**
Art Director: Basil Pao
Client: Atlantic Records

438
Editorial
Artist: **Barbara Nessim**
Art Director: Art Kane
Publication: Viva Magazine

439
Editorial
Artist: **Ken Dallison**
Art Director: Charles O. Hyman
Publication: National Geographic

So they went along and they went
along until they met Foxy Loxy.
"Where are you going?" he asked.
"The sky is falling. We are going to
tell the king," they said.
"Ahhh, but you are going the wrong
way," said Foxy Loxy. "I'll show you
where to go. Come with me."

440
Book
Artist: **Barry Zaid**
Art Director: Eleanor Ehrhardt
Title: Chicken Little
Publisher: Random House, Inc.
Gold Medal

441
Editorial
Artist: **Doug Johnson**
Art Director: Bert Sugar
Publication: Argosy Magazine

442
Editorial
Artist: **Robert Heindel**
Art Director: Joe Sapinsky
Publication: Woman's Day Magazine

443
Editorial
Artist: **Simms Taback**
Art Director: David Barba
Publication: Practical Radiology

Simms Tarach

444
Advertising
Artist: **Jacob Knight**
Art Director: Don Scaglione
Client: Arton Associates, Inc.

445
Advertising
Artist: **Simms Taback**
Art Director: David Barba
Agency: Naimark & Barba, Inc.
Client: Lederle

447
Institutional
Artist: **Gerry Gersten**
Art Director: Gerry Gersten
Client: Art Directors Club of New York

446
Book
Artist: **Edward Soyka**
Art Director: Ian Summers
Title: Noah's Ark
Publisher: Ballantine Books, Inc.

449
Editorial
Artist: **Roy Carruthers**
Art Director: Joe Brooks
Publication: Penthouse Magazine

448
Book
Artist: **Darrell Sweet**
Art Director: Marion Davis
Title: The Other Room
Publisher: The Reader's Digest

450
Editorial
Artist: **Charles Lilly**
Art Director: Ida Lewis
Publication: Encore Magazine

451
Editorial
Artist: **Brad Holland**
Art Director: Ruth Ansel
Publication: The New York Times

452
Book
Artist: **Walter Rane**
Art Director: Rita Cullen
Title: A Textbook of General Psychology
Publisher: Chandler Publishing Co.

453
Advertising
Artist: **Carol Anthony**
Art Director: Andrew Kner
Client: The New York Times

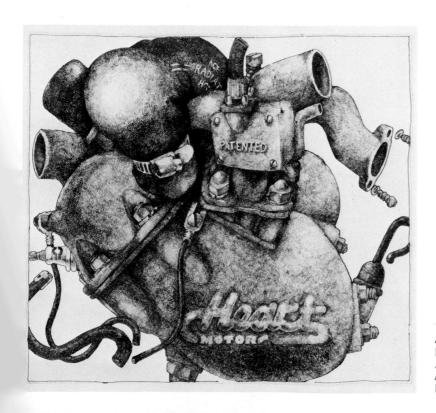

454
Editorial
Artist: **David A. Johnson**
Art Director: Ira Silberlicht/Tom Lennon
Publication: Emergency Medicine

455
Book
Artist: **Jim Sharpe**
Art Director: Thomas Von Der Linn
Title: The Guns of Navarone
Publisher: The Reader's Digest

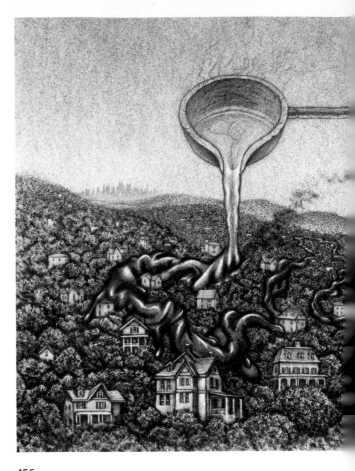

456
Editorial
Artist: **Edward Soyka**
Art Director: Ira Silberlicht/Tom Lennon
Publication: Emergency Medicine

457
Advertising
Artist: **Paul Melia**
Art Director: Wes Highmiller
Agency: H-H Art Studios, Inc.
Client: Teleflora Inc.

458
Advertising
Artist: **Tony Chen**
Art Director: Joseph Stelmach
Client: RCA Records

459
Institutional
Artist: **John Collier**
Art Director: Sam Beeson
Agency: Kelvin Group Partnership
Client: Service Corporation International

460
Editorial
Artist: **Doug Johnson**
Art Director: Don Menell
Publication: Oui Magazine

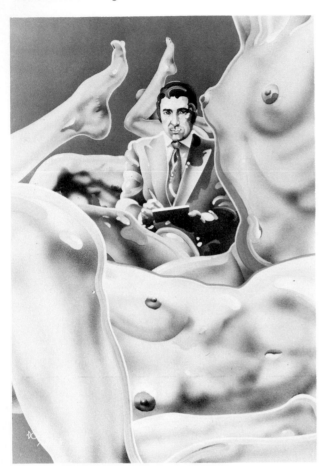

461
Editorial
Artist: **David Wilcox**
Art Director: Norman S. Hotz
Publication: Travel & Leisure

462
Editorial
Artist: **Nicholas Gaetano**
Art Director: Joan Fenton
Publication: New Ingenue Magazine

463
Editorial
Artist: **John Keely**
Art Director: Dennis Ku
Publication: Amoco Oil Co. Magazine

464
Editorial
Artist: **Gene Wilkes**
Art Director: Joe Brooks/Leo McCarthy
Publication: Penthouse Magazine

465
Advertising
Artist: **Jerry Pinkney**
Art Director: Elmer Pizzi
Agency: Gray & Rogers, Inc.
Client: Grit

466
Book
Artist: **William S. Shields**
Art Director: Edward A. Hamilton
Title: The English Tradition: Fiction
Publisher: MacMillan Publishing Co., Inc.

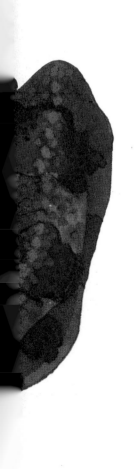

467
Advertising
Artist: **Robert C. Kinyon**
Art Director: Robert Perine
Agency: Frye & Smith, Ltd.
Client: Sidney Foster

469
Advertising
Artist: **Anna Marie Magagna**
Art Director: Anna Marie Magagna

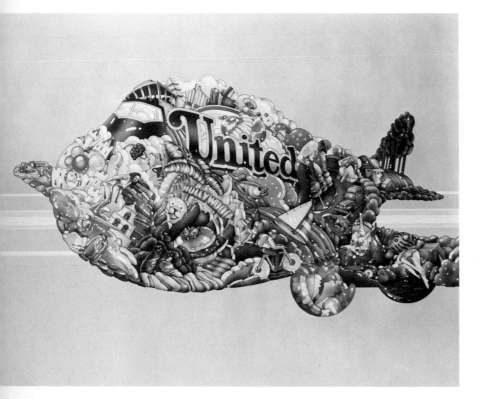

468
Advertising
Artist: **Doug Johnson**
Art Director: Bud Watts
Agency: Leo Burnett Co., Inc.
Client: United Airlines

470
Advertising
Artist: **Patti Churchill**
Art Director: Hank Carocelli
Agency: McCann-Erickson Inc.
Client: Buick Motor Division

471
Advertising
Artist: **Howard Terpning**
Art Director: Jerry Baker
Agency: Cunningham & Walsh
Client: Pendleton Woolen Mills

472
Advertising
Artist: **Paul Giovanopoulos**
Art Director: B. Martin Pedersen
Agency: Pedersen Design, Inc.
Client: Volkswagen

473
Institutional
Artist: **Tina Fritsche**
Art Director: Sharon Stolzenberger
Client: Gibson Greeting Cards

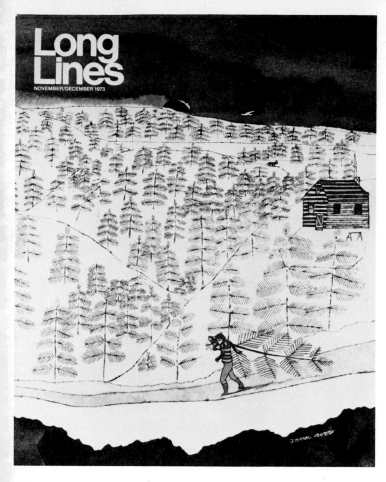

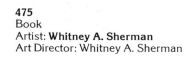

474
Editorial
Artist: **Frank Bozzo**
Art Director: Kim Armstrong/Bob Eichiagen
Publication: Long Lines—AT&T

475
Book
Artist: **Whitney A. Sherman**
Art Director: Whitney A. Sherman

476
Editorial
Artist: **Robert LoGrippo**
Art Director: Robert LoGrippo

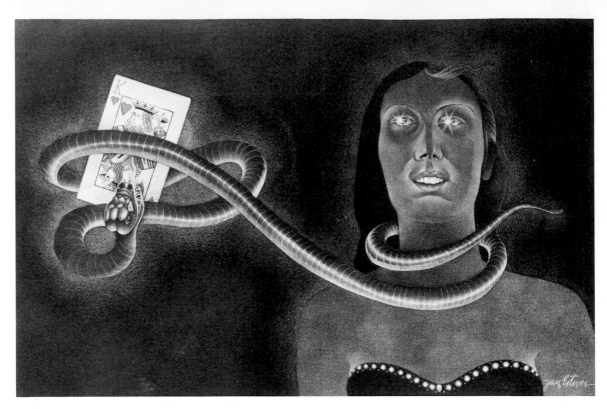

477
Editorial
Artist: **Jan Estevas**
Art Director: Joe Connolly
Publication: Genesis Magazine

478
Advertising
Artist: **Miriam Schottland**
Art Director: Fred S. Pelczar
Agency: Advance Group, Inc.
Client: International Paper Co.

479
Book
Artist: **Robert Giusti**
Art Director: Lynn Braswell
Title: The Forests of the Night
Publisher: The Dial Press

481
Editorial
Artist: **Marvin Friedman**
Art Director: Joe Sapinsky
Publication: Woman's Day Magazine

480
Book
Artist: **Alan Magee**
Art Director: Milton Charles
Title: The Lion of Boaz
Publisher: Pocket Books

482
Book
Artist: **D. Gary Cooley**
Art Director: Jerry Pruiett
Publisher: Onoma Productions

483
Book
Artist: **Karl Swanson**
Art Director: Ian Summers
Title: Paul Bunyan
Publisher: Ballantine Books, Inc.

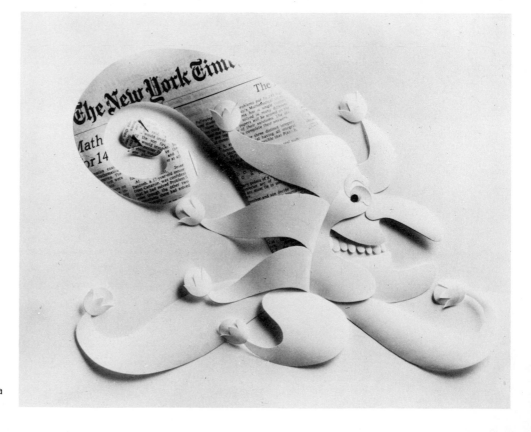

484
Advertising
Artist: **Oni**
Art Director: Andrew Kner/Emil Micha
Client: The New York Times

485
Editorial
Artist: **Stuart Kaufman**
Art Director: William F. Cadge
Publication: Redbook

486
Advertising
Artist: **Christopher Spollen**
Art Director: Christopher Spollen

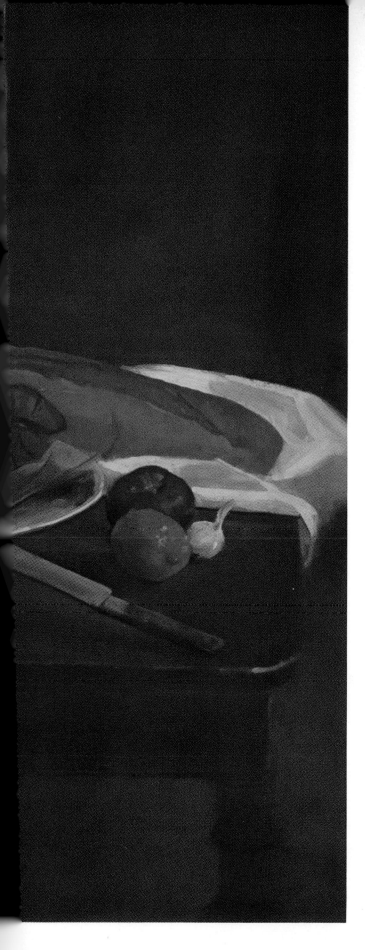

487
Advertising
Artist: **Bernard P. Colonna**
Art Director: Fred S. Pelczar
Client: International Paper Co.

488
Editorial
Artist: **Siegbert Reinhard**
Art Director: Seigbert Reinhard

489
Advertising
Artist: **Robert Byrd**
Art Director: Elmer Pizzi
Agency: Gray & Rogers, Inc.
Client: Grit

490
Advertising
Artist: **Bruce Wolfe**
Art Director: Chris Blum
Agency: Honig, Cooper & Harrington
Client: Levi-Strauss

491
Book
Artist: **Neal Adams**
Art Director: Ian Summers
Title: The Return of Tarzan
Publisher: Ballantine Books, Inc.

493
Institutional
Artist: **Ted CoConis**
Art Director: Ted CoConis

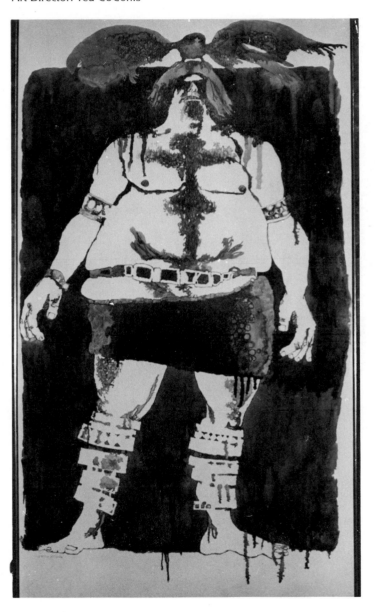

492
Book
Artist: **Seigbert Reinhard**
Art Director: Eleanor Thayer
Title: Worms
Publisher: D.C. Heath & Co.

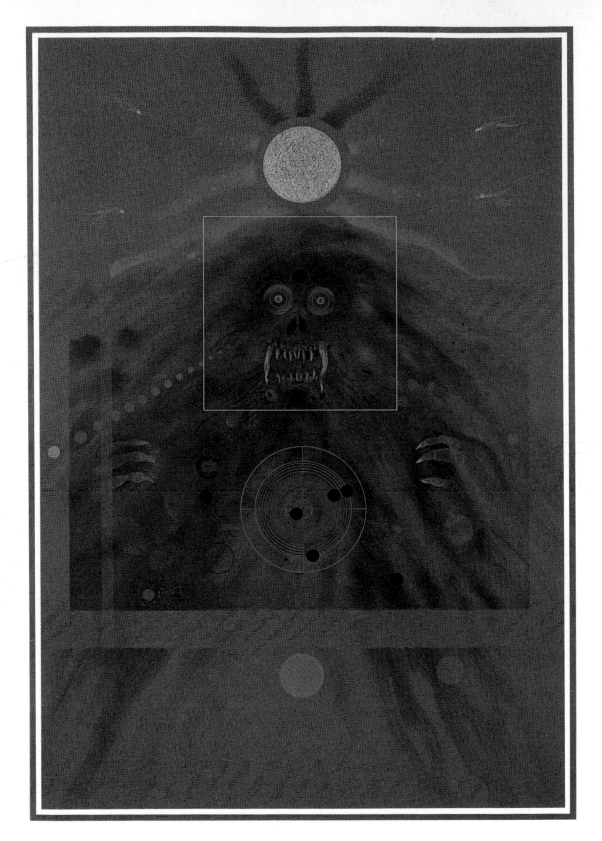

494
Editorial
Artist: **Terry Steadham**
Art Director: Lawrence Timmons
Publication: Young World

495
Book
Artist: **Herb Tauss**
Art Director: Milton Charles
Title: Endless Night
Publisher: Pocket Books
Award of Excellence

497
Advertising
Artist: **Elwyn Mehlman**
Art Director: Bob Kwait
Agency: Griswold-Eshelman
Client: Industry Week

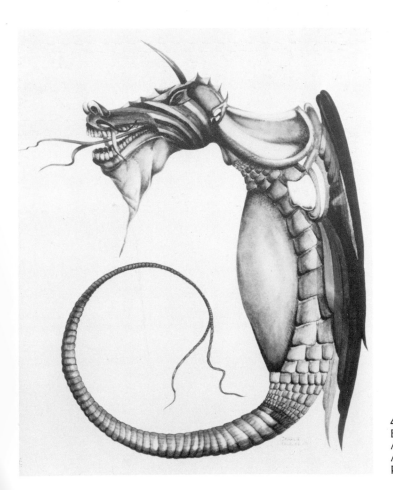

496
Editorial
Artist: **Charles Taublieb**
Art Director: Charles Taublieb
Publication: True Magazine

498
Institutional
Artist: **Albino Hinojosa**
Art Director: Albino Hinojosa

500
Editorial
Artist: **Charles B. Slackman**
Art Director: Ken Munowitz
Publication: Horizon Magazine

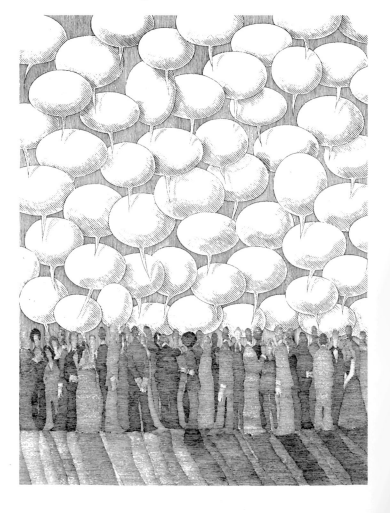

499
Book
Artist: **Mark Livingston**
Art Director: Earl Tidwell
Title: An Everyday History of Somewhere
Publisher: Random House, Inc.

502
Editorial
Artist: **Fran Otnes**
Art Director: Robert Hallock
Publication: Lithopinion

501
Advertising
Artist: **Karen Laurence**
Art Director: Don Scaglione
Client: Arton Associates, Inc.

503
Editorial
Artist: **Donald A. Mackay**
Art Director: Howard E. Paine
Publication: National Geographic

504
Editorial
Artist: **Don Troiani**
Art Director: Emma Landau
Publication: American Heritage

505
Book
Artist: **David Blossom**
Art Director: Thomas Von Der Linn
Title: I, Benedict Arnold
Publisher: The Reader's Digest

507
Book
Artist: **Harry J. Schaare**
Art Director: Harry J. Schaare

508
Advertising
Artist: **Jerry Karl**
Art Director: Jerry Karl
Client: The New Studio Inc.

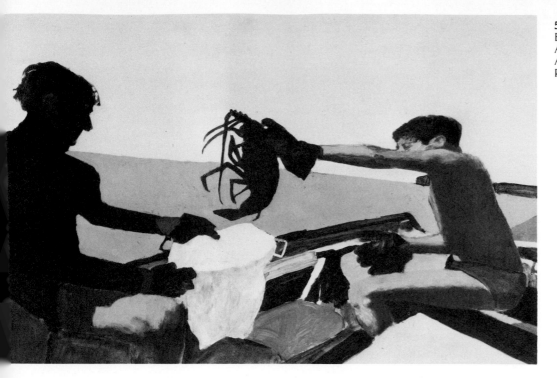

509
Editorial
Artist: **Robert M. Cunningham**
Art Director: B. Martin Pedersen
Publication: Pastimes Magazine

510
Book
Artist: **Richard Amundsen**
Art Director: Frances Giannoni
Title: Whales, Friendly Dolphins & Mighty
    Giants of the Sea
Publisher: Western Publishing Co., Inc.

511
Advertising
Artist: **Robert L. Bender**
Art Director: Robert L. Bender
Client: Lord, Sullivan & Yoder Advertising

512
Book
Artist: **Lou Brooks**
Art Director: Zlata Paces/Kramer Miller/
  Lomden Glassman
Title: Some Who Flew
Publisher: Macmillan Publishing Co., Inc.

513
Editorial
Artist: **Bart Forbes**
Art Director: Tom Ries
Publication: The American Way

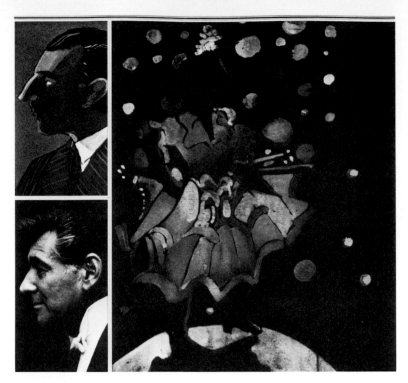

515
Advertising
Artist: **Robert Andrew Parker**
Art Director: John Berg
Client: CBS Records

514
Advertising
Artist: **Margaret Cusack**
Art Director: Leonard Restivo
Client: Bloomingdale's

516
Advertising
Artist: **Robert Pryor**
Art Director: Teresa Alfieri
Client: CBS Records

517
Film
Artist: **Bob Peak/Marcy Gold**
Producer: Carnig Ermoyan
Director: Bob Blansky
Production Company: Dolphin Productions
Client: Warner Bros., Inc.
Award for Excellence

518
Advertising
Artist: **Robert Weaver**
Art Director: Richard Wilde
Client: School of Visual Arts

519
Book
Artist: **Lee Rosenblatt**
Art Director: Ian Summers
Title: House of Cards
Publisher: Ballantine Books, Inc.

520
Institutional
Artist: **E. Stephen Perry**
Art Director: Fred Alves
Client: Hoffmann-La Roche Inc.

521
Advertising
Artist: **Robert Giusti**
Art Director: Joseph Stelmach
Client: RCA Records

522
Book
Artist: **Herbert L. Fink**
Art Director: Betty Anderson
Title: The King's Indian
Publisher: Random House, Inc.

523
Editorial
Artist: **Jean Michel Folon**
Art Director: Phillip Dykstra
Publication: Modern Medicine

524
Book
Artist: **William S. Shields**
Art Director: Edward A. Hamilton
Title: The English Tradition: Poetry
Publisher: Macmillan Publishing Co., Inc.

525
Artist: **James McMullan**
Advertising
Art Director: Richard Wilde
Client: School of Visual Arts

526
Advertising
Artist: **Robert Andrew Parker**
Art Director: John Berg
Client: CBS Records

527
Book
Artist: **John Berkey**
Art Director: Vince Maiello
Title: The Glass Inferno
Publisher: Doubleday & Co., Inc.

528
Book
Artist: **Reynold Ruffins**
Art Director: Alan Benjamin
Title: The 1975 Riddle Calendar
Publisher: Charles Scribner's Sons

What bolt is never on a door? A thunderbolt.

What kind of paper should be used to make a kite?

Flypaper.

Where does Sunday come before Thursday? In the dictionary

Why is a March weather forecast like a baby? Because it's always being changed.

Who shoots people, blows them up, and lets them go home and hang themselves? A photographer.

What is everyone in the world doing at the same time? Getting older.

529
Advertising
Artist: **D. R. Shuck**
Art Director: D. R. Shuck
Client: The Wire Wheel

530
Book
Artist: **Robert Grossman**
Art Director: Ian Summers
Title: Boys On The Bus
Publisher: Ballantine Books, Inc.

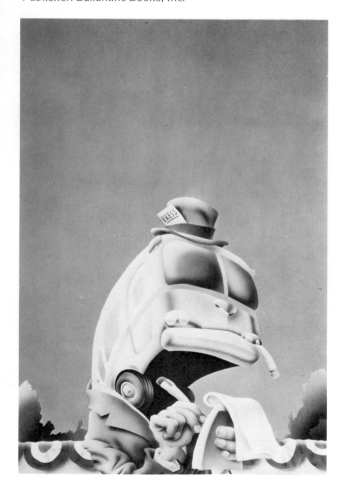

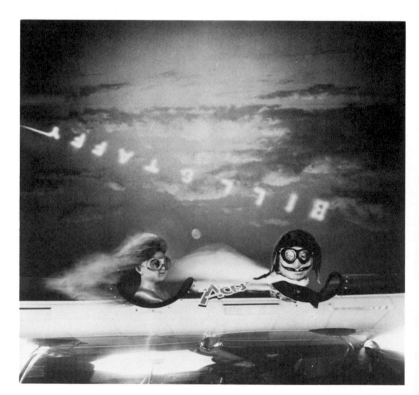

531
Advertising
Artist: **Craig DeCamps**
Art Director: Ace Lehman
Client: RCA Records

532
Book
Artist: **Robert Byrd**
Art Director: Robert Kraus/Riki Levenson
Title: Rebecca Hatpin
Publisher: Windmill Books/E. P. Dutton & Co., Inc.

533
Advertising
Artist: **D. R. Shuck**
Art Director: D. R. Shuck
Client: The Wire Wheel

534
Advertising
Artist: **Dennis Pohl**
Art Director: Dennis Pohl
Client: ESP Disk

537
Advertising
Artist: **Mark English**
Art Director: Frank Wagner
Agency: Sudler & Hennessey, Inc.
Client: Pfizer Laboratories

535
Advertising
Artist: **Allan Mardon**
Art Director: Ward Emerson
Agency: Fairfax Advertising
Client: Water Tower Place

536
Book
Artist: **Robert Heindel**
Art Director: Thomas Von Der Linn
Title: Casino Royale
Publisher: The Reader's Digest

538
Editorial
Artist: **Fred Otnes**
Art Director: Robert Hallock
Publication: Lithopinion

539
Institutional
Artist: **James McMullan**
Art Director: David Turill
Agency: McCann-Erickson, Inc.
Client: Unigard Insurance Co.

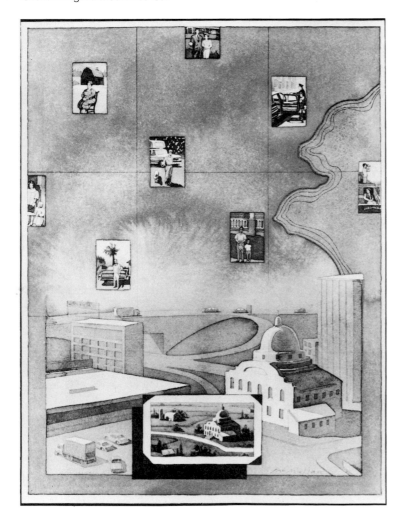

540
Book
Artist: **Mark S. Fisher**
Art Director: Mark S. Fisher

ILLUSTRATORS 17

ROY MILLER, JR.
ADVERTISING ART

5378 HAZELHURST STREET • PHILADELPHIA, PENNSYLVANIA 19131

The name Lavaty has stood behind outstanding art for over 30 years.

You'll find contemporary and nostalgic styles treating all subjects. Individual portfolios are available from the following artists represented exclusively by Frank and Jeff Lavaty.

John Berkey, Don Daily, Bernard D'Andrea, Roland Descombes, Chris Duke, Lorraine Fox, Gervasio Gallardo, Martin Hoffman, Stan Hunter, Chet Jezierski, Mort Kunstler, Lemuel Line, Robert Logrippo, Charles Moll, Carlos Ochagavia, Robert Schulz.

Contact Frank & Jeff Lavaty for free color booklet.

Representative booklet of 100 color examples available for your file. Phone (212) 355-0910. Or write Frank and Jeff Lavaty, 45 East 51st St., N.Y., N.Y. 10022.

ART & ILLUSTRATION

ART

FRANK & JEFF LAVATY—ARTIST REPRESENTATIVES
45 EAST 51st STREET, N.Y., N.Y. 22 PHONE 212-355-0910

GERALD & CULLEN RAPP, INC.
251 EAST 51 STREET • NYC 10022
PHONE: (212) 751-4656

ILLUSTRATORS' AGENTS

ALAN E. COBER

REPRESENTED BY CULLEN RAPP 251 E. 51 ST., NEW YORK 10022: PL 1-4656

BOB DESCHAMPS

Represented by:
GERALD &
CULLEN RAPP, Inc.
251 East 51 Street
New York, 10022
212 PLaza 1-4656

RAY DOMINGO

Represented by:
CULLEN RAPP, Inc.
251 East 51 Street, New York, N.Y.
212 PLaza 1-4656

GERRY GERSTEN

Represented by:
GERALD & CULLEN RAPP
251 East 51 Street
New York, N.Y. 10022
212 PLaza 1-4656

SHARON KNETTELL

Represented by: GERALD & CULLEN RAPP
251 East 51 Street, New York, N.Y. 10022
212 PLaza 1-4656

GINNIE HOFMANN

Represented by: GERALD & CULLEN RAPP, Inc.
251 East 51 Street, New York, N.Y. 10022
212 PLaza 1-4656

MARIE MICHAL

Represented by:
GERALD & CULLEN RAPP, Inc.
251 East 51 Street
New York, N.Y. 10022
212 PLaza 1-4656

GARY OVERACRE

Represented by:
GERALD & CULLEN RAPP, Inc
251 East 51 Street
New York, N.Y. 10022
212 PLaza 1-4656

LOU MYERS

JERRY PINKNEY

Represented by:
GERALD & CULLEN RAPP, Inc.
212 PLaza 1 4656

LIONEL KALISH

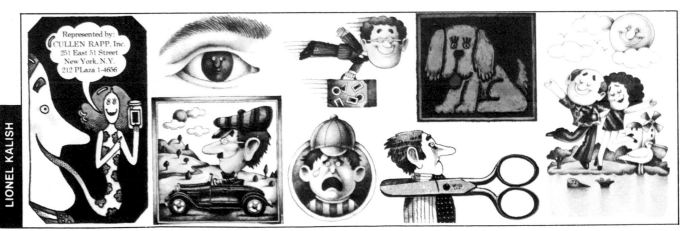

Represented by:
CULLEN RAPP, Inc.
251 East 51 Street
New York, N.Y.
212 PLaza 1-4656

SIEGBERT REINHARD

Represented by:
GERALD &
CULLEN RAPP, Inc.
251 East 51 Street
New York, 10022
212 PLaza 1-4656

We have
an opening
for one
additional
great
illustrator

GERALD & CULLEN RAPP, INC.
251 EAST 51 STREET • NYC 10022
PHONE: (212) 751-4656

PETER PALOMBI

Represented by:
GERALD & CULLEN RAPP, Inc.
212 PLaza 1-4656

Jessie Neeley

JESSIE NEELEY ARTIST REPRESENTATIVE 575-1234

art staff inc.

An Advertising & Design Service

369 Lexington Ave., New York, N.Y. 10017 • (212) 867-2660

We thank all the fine talent that contributed to our publications during this past year:

Jim Alexander
Anographics Inc.
Don Bolognese
Adolph E. Brotman
Gerry Contreras
Farmlett, Barsanti Inc.
Nicholas Fasciano
Susan Fox
Dale Gustafson
Michael A. Hampshier
Michael Henning
Walter Kacik Design Associates
George Kelvin
Jerome Kuhl
Roger Metcalf
Oni
Kurt Ortell
Rafael D. Palacios
Michael Ramus
Gerhard Richter
John Sagan
Bert Silverman
Raymond Skibinski
Stasolla & Tesoro Inc.
William G. Teodecki
Dan Todd
Guy Tudor
Ed Valigursky
Vantage Art Inc.
Jim Whitman Studio
Fred Wolff
Patricia J. Wynne

TIME-LIFE BOOKS, Time & Life Building, Rockefeller Center, New York, N.Y. 10020
Telephone 212-556-2356

OUR TEN COMMANDMENTS
OF ARTIST REPRESENTATION

1. We represent only artists we believe in and are totally committed to them.

2. We believe in being more than agents and become involved in the <u>total career</u> of the artists we represent.

3. We appreciate the problems of the artist and try, whenever possible, to alleviate these problems.

4. We also appreciate the problems of the art director: his client-agency relationship, tight deadlines and budget limitations and try to help him solve these problems whenever we can.

5. We believe in <u>full representation</u>. That means taking on only that number of artists that we can fully represent as well as insuring that each artist is non-competitive in style with other artists we represent.

6. We believe in giving <u>full service</u> to our artists and to the art director, promptly and professionally. Every client, no matter what the job price, deserves the very best we can offer.

7. We believe in being <u>flexible</u>. Business conditions change. The economy rises and falls. Accounts switch. We and our artists must adjust to all changes in order to successfully survive.

8. We believe in always meeting deadlines and always keeping a bargain. We and our artists are only as good as our word and our last job.

9. We believe in BEING HONEST at all times. With our artists. With the art director. With ourselves.

10. And finally, we believe in our <u>profession</u> . . . the profession of representing artists. We firmly believe that it is the most exciting and challenging profession anywhere and we are proud to be a part of it.

Barbara Gordon
Associates Ltd.
165 East 32 Street
New York, N.Y. 10016
212-686-3514

SEND SAMPLES OF YOUR WORK TO:

**EDITORIAL ART DEPARTMENT, 10TH FLOOR
PLAYBOY MAGAZINE
919 NORTH MICHIGAN AVENUE
CHICAGO, ILLINOIS 60611**

KEEP THE BEST AT YOUR FINGERTIPS!

GRAPHIS ANNUAL '75/'76
International Advertising and Editorial Graphics

Edited by Walter Herdeg. The 24th annual edition of the collection that the *AIGA Journal* calls "a visual feast." Here's the best work from all over the world in advertisements, booklets, magazine covers, trademarks, and film and television. 250 pages, 9½" x 12", 1000 illustrations, 80 in full color, indexes.

GRAPHIS POSTERS '76
The International Annual of Poster Art

Edited by Walter Herdeg. The fourth edition of this annual again presents an informative cross-section of international production in the various fields of poster art. The sections are arranged according to Decorative posters, Advertising posters, Cultural posters, and Social posters. 220 pages, 9½" x 12", 759 illustrations (108 in color).

PHOTOGRAPHIS '76
The International Annual of Advertising, Editorial and Television Photography

Edited by Walter Herdeg. "Over the past few years, the PHOTOGRAPHIS ANNUAL has become one of the most valuable of the yearly graphic arts publications due to the comprehensiveness of its coverage and the care with which it is reproduced." – CA Magazine. 264 pages, 9½" x 12", about 800 illustrations (80 in color).

EUROPEAN ILLUSTRATION '75/'76
The Second Annual of European Editorial, Book, Advertising, Television, Cinema and Design Art

Edited by Edward Booth-Clibborn. Drawing its material from the widest range of European mass media and from the European publishing business this is an unparalleled showcase for the versatile talents of the leading artists and illustrators at work in Europe today. 256 pages, 9" x 11", 350 subjects (50 in color).

Contact **Carol Bancroft & Friends** 1A Putnam Green Greenwich Connecticut 06830 203 531·1741

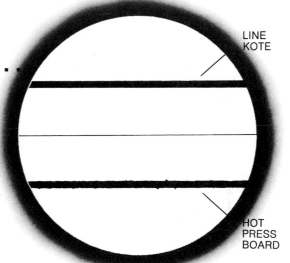
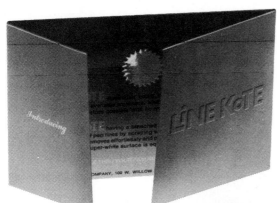

Kirchoff/Wohlberg, Inc.
artists representative

331 East 50 Street, New York, New York 10022   212-753-5146
589 Boston Post Road, Madison, Connecticut 06443   203-245-7308

Bernie Fuchs, Alan E. Cober, Bob Heindel, Robert Peak, Fred Otnes, Mark English

**6 of todays great illustrators
invite 150 of tomorrows great illustrators
to join The Illustrators Workshop**

Working illustrators and advanced
students are invited to take part in an
exciting 4-week work/study session.

There's only room for 150. Each will work
closely with the pros pictured above.
The best knowledge available...yours
for a month.

For all details, including when, where
and how much, write:
The Illustrators Workshop
P.O. Box 280, Easton, CT. 06425

artists

Norman Adams, Kevin Brooks
David Byrd, John Collier
Norman La Liberte, Dennis Luczak
Jim Manos, Allan Mardon, John Martin
Fred Otnes, Gene Szafran.

Represented by:
Bill Erlacher, Artists Associates
211 East 51 Street, New York, N.Y. 10022
Telephone: (212) 755-1365/6
Associates: David Cross
Alan Spitzer, Arlene Reiss

ILLUSTRATORS 17

Index

While every effort has been made to insure the accuracy of the credits in this volume, it is inevitable that an occasional error may have crept in. On behalf of the Society of Illustrators, the publishers would appreciate any information about any omissions or corrections. As this book is printed in process colors, we regret that the original colors of some of the illustrations reproduced here have been altered.

Production Credits

The text in this book is:
Korinna with Bold
Composition by: M. J. Baumwell;
Typography
Offset plates and printing by:
Connecticut Printers, Inc.
The paper is: Mead's Black and
White Offset Enamel Dull
Paper supplier: Andrews/Nelson/
Whitehead Publishing Papers
Binding cloth by:
G. S. B. Fabrics Corp.
Bound by: A. Horowitz and Son
Jacket printed by:
Princeton Polychrome Press
Production Supervision:
Lee Tobin, Hastings House
Assistant to the publisher:
James Moore, Hastings House

INDEX

ILLUSTRATORS

Wozniak, Dorothy, 248
601 Rockwell
Cleveland, OH

Wozniak, Elaine, 372
601 Rockwell
Cleveland, OH

Zagorski, Stanislaw, 216
c/o Atlantic Records
75 Rockefeller Place
New York City

Zaid, Barry, 440
c/o Push Pin Studio
207 East 32 Street
New York City

Ziemienski, Dennis, 397
244 Emerson Street
Palo Alto, CA

Zimmerman, Marie, 147
1264 Ogden
Denver, CO

ART DIRECTORS

FILM DIRECTORS

FILM PHOTOGRAPHY

FILM PRODUCERS

FILM PRODUCTION,
see under **AGENCIES**

CLIENTS

TITLES